The Last Word

The Last Word

AN AUTOBIOGRAPHY

Quentin Crisp

Edited by Phillip Ward
and
Laurence Watts

Front cover photograph by Joseph Mulligan

ISBN-13: 9780692968482
ISBN-10: 0692968482

Foreword

THE LAST WORD IS THE third installment of Quentin Crisp's autobiography. Let's start there. What kind of a man gets to write three autobiographies? Most of us will never get to write one. Moreover, what kind of man achieves fame, or infamy as Quentin would say, in his sixties?

The answer is a man who was universally shunned and who became famous for revealing his society-enforced exile to the world. It took Quentin the vast majority of his life to generate the kind of "life experience" that would eventually fill the pages of *The Naked Civil Servant*. Was it time well spent? Hardly. But Quentin was, in more ways than one, very much a victim of the time in which he lived.

Homosexuality was illegal in the United Kingdom until 1967, by which time Quentin was 58 years old, ten years after the Wolfendon report had recommended that homosexual behavior between consenting adults in private should no longer be a criminal offence. Quentin's seminal radio interview with Phillip O'Connor may have been broadcast in 1964, but the first installment of his autobiography, *The Naked Civil*

Servant, was not published until 1968. Public interest in the book's subject matter would surely have been key to Jonathan Cape's decision to commission the work.

A year later the Stonewall riots took place in New York, followed over the next several years by the state by state repeal of the majority of America's sodomy laws. *The Naked Civil Servant* rode this wave of liberalism, becoming a television documentary in 1971 and a film in 1975 starring John Hurt as Quentin, a performance for which he won the 1976 British Academy of Film and Television Arts (BAFTA) Award for Best Actor.

The Naked Civil Servant elevated Quentin Crisp to the status of gay icon, detailing as it did Quentin's pioneering existence and persecution as an openly gay man in the 1930s, 40s, 50s and 60s. It was very much a first of its kind. Was Quentin the kind of gay icon that the emerging global gay community wanted or needed? Perhaps not, but who else was there? Initially at least, options were few. Gay men may not have looked at Quentin and seen themselves, but they related to his isolation and oppression.

What Quentin did next however was perpetuate his celebrity through an eccentricity and constant accessibility that kept him on the fringes of the art and entertainment worlds for the next twenty-four years. To be fair, he never achieved Hollywood-level fame, but the suffering of his early life gave him a credibility that endeared him to the gay community and a number of influential people.

One of Crisp's fans was Sting who wrote his 1987 hit *Englishman in New York* about him. Another was Calvin Klein who cast Quentin in a commercial for one of his colognes. The list goes on and meant that the pain of Quentin's early years was at least partially compensated for in the twilight of his life. Shear longevity on Crisp's part meant that he was able to enjoy this cult status for years more than a typical actor or writer. In fact, by the time he died in 1999 Quentin had published 14 books and starred in more than 20 films despite no specific training in either craft.

The Last Word reads differently from Quentin's earlier books, especially *The Naked Civil Servant*. This owes less to how it has been edited and more to when and how it was written. Quentin lost the use of his left hand in the early 1990s when he was in his eighties and became unable to use his typewriter. Subsequent works of his were dictated; *The Last Word* was recorded by his best friend Phillip Ward. As such, *The Last Word* reads more like a monologue and less like a written text. We have tried to alter the content and style of *The Last Word* as little as possible in the hope that the end result provides a more reliable and intimate portrait of Quentin in the last year of his life. Yes, he grandstands and repeats and contradicts himself, but what ninety-year-old that you know doesn't? The important thing is that he is speaking directly to you because as you read this you are the most important person in the world to him.

This final installment of his autobiography was finished in 1999, the year of Quentin's death. As you'll see from reading this book, Quentin had begun to put his affairs in order knowing that, aged ninety and with an enlarged heart and prostate cancer, his long life was finally nearing its end. He didn't know exactly how much longer he had, but *The Last Word* was written to share his untold stories and to reflect for the last time on an extraordinary life.

Why has it taken so long to be published? Well, perhaps that's what happens when you leave your best friend in charge of your literary estate. As I mentioned, Quentin dictated this book to Phillip. When one listens to the recordings as I have, Quentin does not sound in good health. Frequently he can be heard coughing or furiously scratching at his cracked and brittle skin. After Quentin's death it was too painful for Phillip to hear Quentin's voice, let alone take in and transcribe what he had said. Time is the only remedy for such pain and that alone explains the delay in getting this book to you.

I first met Phillip when I interviewed him for *Pink News* in 2011. Once our interview had been published he enlisted me to help him with *The Last Word* and our combined efforts have produced the text you are about to read. One of my regrets is that we were unable to finish it before John Hurt's death earlier this year. Another issue is that, with so much time having passed since Quentin's death, there is the very real question of just how many people now remember who Quentin was. It is with this in mind, not to mention the generational collapse in reading that we are currently witnessing, that I have sought to provide as much detail on Quentin's life, observations and quotes in the form of footnotes. I have assumed little to no knowledge of Quentin's reference points on the part of the reader.

Quentin, as I have said, was a victim of his time in more ways than one. This is particularly true when it comes to his transgenderism which he talks about at length in *The Last Word*. That Quentin lived his life believing himself to be gay is because our understanding of what it means to be transgender is relatively new. The term itself only acquired its current meaning in the 1990s, the last decade of Quentin's life. He mistook being transgender for being homosexual in the same way that Chaz Bono, the erstwhile daughter of Cher, first believed he was lesbian. The gay men who couldn't associate with Quentin's femininity or his pronouncements about gay life were right to be confused. He inaccurately believed his own feelings were the same as theirs. It turns out they weren't.

Crisp's other altercations with the gay community arguably came about because of his assumed later-in-life role of quotable contrarian, which kept his name in the news and no doubt kept the dinner invitations rolling in. Quentin had two strings to his public commentary bow. When it came to talking about himself he told you what you wanted to hear: that he was unloved, that England was horrible, that everyone and everything in America was wonderful, and that he had never worked a day in his life. When it came to talking about other people, topics or events, he erred towards sensationalism. This made sure that his was the quote the journalists printed. Even if it wasn't actually his opinion. Thus, "Princess Diana was a disgrace who got what she deserved" and "AIDS was a fad." These so-called "opinions" of Quentin's became problems for him that were further complicated by his refusal to publicly recant anything he had previously said. Doing so, he thought, would cost him credibility.

It is true of course that Quentin was surrounded by love, and he expressed his own love to those close to him. Despite his earlier condemnation of England, he was grateful to it for giving him fame. He fully realized that America is as littered with pockets of bigotry and homophobia as other developed nations are. He ended his life with more acting credits than most actors have, more books published than most writers achieve, and with more than a million dollars in the bank. Quentin however never let the facts get in the way of a good anecdote.

Phillip Ward has kindly provided an afterword to *The Last Word* which serves as the final chapter to this book. He was the person closest to Quentin and hence is most able to recount Crisp's last days.

Finally, let me turn to Quentin's legacy. *The Naked Civil Servant* remains Quentin's most important work and in it he details for future generations what it was like to be openly gay during a time when homosexuality was considered immoral and was in fact illegal. The book and film of the same name provided hope for those living in an age of now legal homosexuality, but who were still subject to discrimination because of society's prejudices.

Quentin's story is one of triumph over adversity, though Crisp can be said to have outlasted his foes rather than having directly fought them. His may not have been a life that you wanted to emulate, his may not have been a look that you wanted to copy, but in the latter part of his life he was an openly gay man who hadn't been imprisoned and broken like Oscar Wilde, who didn't take his life like Alan Turing, who wasn't associated with "boys" like Bill Tilden, who didn't remain closeted like E. M. Forster or John Maynard Keynes, who wasn't disgraced like John Gielgud and who didn't succumb to AIDS like Rock Hudson.

Here was an openly gay man who put up with what the world threw at him, lived to a grand old age and who found relative fame and eventually fortune at the age of sixty, seventy, eighty and even ninety. His sheer existence told gay men in Britain, America and throughout the world that they were not alone and that there is always hope.

Laurence Watts
August 2017

CHAPTER 1

Sex, Sexuality and Identity

THIS WILL BE THE LAST book that I write. What little I can say and do is almost done because, at the end of the day, I am nobody and I am nothing.

Most of my life is contained within the pages of *The Naked Civil Servant* and *How To Become A Virgin*. The former deals with my so-called life in England and the latter with my rebirth here in America. I only have a few more stories left to share before my well runs dry. I know and hope that the end is near. This book will be my swan song. A chance for me to have the last word.

It is my opinion that everyone should write at least one book in their lifetime and that if a person writes just one book then it should be a book about themselves and in it they should tell the truth. He or she should not be held back by the fact that they can't write or that they can't make the subject matter picturesque. That's a mistake. Miss Stein[1] said, "The way to say it is to say it." And she spoke the truth.

---

1 Gertrude Stein, American novelist, poet and playwright, 1874-1946

Where then should I begin? I'll begin with my truth, at the very beginning.

When I was writing *The Naked Civil Servant* I remember Mr. Carroll[2] saying to me, "Don't say too much about your childhood. I'm bored with people's childhoods." I have to say that I failed him. The truth is I had to try and understand why I had been such a wretched child. I was a terrible nuisance and wanted attention more than anything.

Later, I met a woman to whom I said, "If all my family had stood around me as a child and said, 'You're wonderful. You're wonderful. You're wonderful.' after an hour I would have complained, 'You're not saying it *loud enough.*'"

And quick as a flash she told me, "My son's like that."

I don't feel uncomfortable about my early life, but it's almost like speaking about another person. It was so long ago it feels like another reality, as if it didn't happen. I can't recall precise feelings that I had, but I can recall facts and sometimes the look of places and people. This lack of sentimentality when remembering the past is one of the few masculine traits I believe I possess.

I don't think there was a single event or thought in my life which shaped who I am today, but there was one long daydream that I lived in, up until at least the age of eleven or twelve. So let us begin this book with that daydream.

I can remember my mother alternately trying to jolt me out of my dream and pandering to my being in it. She even

---

2 Donald Carroll, Quentin's literary agent, 1940-2010

bought me ballet shoes. Now, I regard this fact as remarkable because I've never since heard of a man wearing blocked toe shoes. I went to a dance class once, in my ballet shoes, and walked up and down the room on my points. I don't remember the mistresses stopping me, or laughing, or anything like that, but looking back it was clearly a sign of things to come.

In my early years I attended a school for boys and girls. Every day the boys would march out onto the field to play football. I refused to play. They would kick the football at me and I would dodge it. I never once tried to kick it in any way. I was preoccupied with my daydream. I suppose my mother must have given up and thought, "Well, that's just the way it is."

When I was very young, my mother read romantic poems to me. She recited *Idylls of the King* by Mr. Tennyson[3] and the narrative poems of Mr. Scott,[4] which very few have heard of. Scott's poems included tales like *The Lady of the Lake* and *Marmion* which inspired me to dream about fair ladies and brave knights, fostering my romantic inner life and shaping my daydream.

I began writing my own poetry. One day my sister and my mother found it and read it. Despite knowing it wasn't for public reading they nevertheless laughed at it, which hurt me a great deal. My sister was malicious. She would say of me, "Oh, he likes to be different."

---

3 Alfred Tennyson, 1st Baron Tennyson, FRS, British poet, 1809-1892
4 Sir Walter Scott, Scottish playwright, novelist and poet, 1771-1832

She never thought, "What is his problem? What can be done about it?" She just thought I was showing off. Of course, I *was* showing off, but at the same time I was in a terrible bind about who and what I was, something she didn't recognize or bother to think about.

My daydream as a child was of growing up to be a very worldly, very beautiful woman. Those were my only daydreams. I played games of make believe with very little girls in the neighborhood. I had no male friends at all. I only had girl friends who could be ruled and made to play parts in my daydreams.

Of course, I never thought I was gay. I never heard the word homosexual until I was about nineteen or twenty, but I knew I was different from other people because they made it perfectly obvious to me. I wasn't worried by it nor did I think, "What shall I do to seem more like a real person?" Somehow, I accepted my fate.

I remember playing a game of make-believe when I was nine or ten with a girl and one of her friends. One of the girls said, "You can be a great, dark prince."

The girl next to her who knew better said, "Oh, Denis[5] never plays the parts of real men."

And I remember thinking, "No, I never do."

And the first girl continued excitedly, "Oh. Well then, *I* will be the great dark prince." It didn't matter to her whether she played a male or female part, it was only a game. To me it

---

5 Quentin Crisp was born Denis Pratt, changing his name in his twenties

4

was more serious than a game however, though I didn't comprehend it at the time.

I never had boy friends because boys wanted to play rough games and sports and I was never any good at those things, so I never was with them. I don't remember ever meeting boys or men and falling in love with them and them kissing my hand or anything like that. I was just always this beautiful creature.

Had I been born a woman, none of my life would have happened and I could have been happy. Well, perhaps that's stretching a point. Let's just say I might not have been quite as unhappy. And of course when you're on the outside looking in, it always seems that other people are happier than you are anyway.

At the age of ninety, it has finally been explained to me that I am not really homosexual, I'm transgender. I now accept that. All my life, I have wanted to be part of society without having to alter my daydream, my own reality. When it comes to sex, these days I'm asexual. Nevertheless, I'm now convinced that it has been my view of myself and not my view of men that has been my trouble.

I no longer see myself as homosexual, though it is a word I have used to describe myself and which others have understandably used to describe me. I don't actually see myself as a man though, of course, I know I'm not physically a woman.

To start, I don't dress like a woman. I did know a man once who worked as a waitress for at least six months and who changed into his uniform in a room where other women were changing and was never detected. That's pretty amazing to me. I don't think I could have done that though. I think my body is too like a man's body to have lived as a woman with any kind of success.

I have also only ever worn drag once. I suppose you could say it was a success in that nothing *happened*. I put on women's clothes, I left the place where I lived, I got on a bus and went to the Regent Palace Hotel, had a drink there with my friend, got on another bus and came back. It was uneventful, but I think I did it to prove to myself that I could live the life of a woman albeit only for a few hours. I don't really know what I expected.

I never came 'out' as transgender or gay because I was never 'in' and I've never known anything except the life I have. I either lived in the dream world in which I was a woman or else I lived awkwardly in the outside world where I was inadequate. The only difference is that now I live my whole life unified by the fact that I can live in the outer world the way I live in my head. I couldn't always do that and it's a freedom I now cherish.

I don't think I ever consciously questioned my sexuality, my identity, my gender, or my daydream. It folded around me rather like the dream of Norma Desmond in *Sunset Boulevard*, the last line of which is, "Life that can be cruel, can also be kind." The dream that meant so much to her finally closed about her. The dream that I am really a woman closed about me entirely. I went through life as though I was a boy in the outer world, but in my head I went on as though I were a woman. This explains why my life has been so strange.

I never went out in the evening thinking, "Now I must get some sex," which nowadays most people do. I went out saying, "I must be my glorious self and it will attract people to me." I didn't want any results. I just wanted to be admired. I think a lot of women think this way. Ms. Dietrich[6] said, "You have to let them put it in, or they don't come back." That's a wonderful thing to have said. She didn't want sex. She wanted admiration, applause and praise. Sex would have smudged her makeup and spoiled her hair.

By accident then, I have become a sort of national hero, or worse (because I now realize its misrepresents me as much as how I managed to misrepresent them) a *gay* national hero. In reality, I was only ever a hopeless case. If I had tried to disguise myself as a real person, everyone would have said, "Who does he think, oh, I beg your pardon, who does *she* think she is?" I never did it and that gave way to the image that I have, the legend, if you will.

Ms. Morris[7], the man who had the operation,[8] once made a wonderful remark. "It was never a question of sex. It was a question of gender."

That's a wonderful thing to have said. He wanted to be a woman. He didn't want to have men so much as to no longer be one, and he succeeded.

The trouble is, of course, that if you have the operation and you tell everyone, you are in as bad a position as you were before

6 Marlene Dietrich, German actress and singer, 1901-1992
7 Jan Morris (formerly James Humphrey Morris), Welsh historian and author b. 1926
8 Known at the time as a sex change

you had it done. Because before you come into the room, people say, "She was really once a man." Then when you arrive, no one can look anywhere except at your face because they can't be seen examining your body to see how different it is.

No one can ask you, "Does it work?" which, of course, is what everyone is longing to know. And then you become peculiar. They expect something special from you and treat you in a special way. The end result of which is you're as removed from real life as you were before, which I would have thought rather defeats the point.

The only thing in my life I have wanted and didn't get was to be a woman. It will be my life's biggest regret. If the operation had been available and cheap when I was young, say when I was twenty-five or twenty-six, I would have jumped at the chance. My life would have been much simpler as a result. I would have told nobody. Instead, I would have gone to live in a distant town and run a knitting wool shop and no one would ever have known my secret. I would have joined the real world and it would have been wonderful.

Having said that, and ignoring the biological impossibility for a moment, I wouldn't have wanted to be a woman with children. I would have accepted children if they somehow came into my life, but the truth is I don't really like children. I am amused when people say to me, "But you were a child once." I was, but I wasn't the kind of child that made you *like* children.

Now, for the rest of this book you will have to forgive me. Having labeled myself homosexual and having been labeled as such by the wider world, I have effectively lived a 'gay' life for most of my years. Consequently, I can relate to gay men because I have more or less been one for so long in spite of my actual fate being that of a woman trapped in a man's body. I refer to myself as homosexual without thinking because of how I have lived my life. If you are reading this and are gay, think of me as one of your own even though you now know the truth. If it's confusing for you, think how confusing it has been for me these past ninety years.

When I was young, I remember swinging about London's West End with my eyelashes blacked and so on, and the other boys would say to me, "Do you find it's any help, all that stuff on your face?"

And I said, "No."

"Well then, why do you do it?" they would ask.

And I would say, "Because I like it. I prefer the way I look now to the way when I wasn't made up."

This they couldn't really understand. If they wore makeup it was to make them look a little younger, or slightly effeminate. This helped them to meet strange men in the street that they could go home with. I didn't want to do that. I wanted to look like myself, or at least more like myself than nature had made me.

A man once asked of me, "If you went to a party and there was someone there more outrageous than yourself, what would you do?"

Flippantly I replied, "Oh, I should scream, or swoon, or both."

He said, "No. I'm serious."

To which I said, "Do you seriously think I would go to all the effort of making myself look like this, and upon finding out that there was someone more outrageous than me at a party that I would leave?"

But he obviously did think that. The truth is I am indifferent to what other people look like.

On one occasion, I was in a room full of people and there was a famous black man there. A woman I know very well said afterwards, "I was terribly worried because I didn't know whether to take you to meet him, or him to meet you."

To which I said, "Do you think I care about that? You think I care whether I'm led to meet somebody famous or whether they are brought to me?"

That's like the notion of having a 'good' table in a restaurant. I wouldn't know what a good table was. I don't expect to be treated in any special way.

So many people misread me or don't understand me. They don't understand how unimportant almost everything is to me except people. In one of the hate letters I received the other day it said, "I understand you now. You're a lonely embittered old queen and you're interested in nothing that matters to other people." And I smiled and thought, "How true." Well, to be honest I didn't understand the word 'embittered' because I would have said I was less embittered than most people, but it's true I'm not interested in the things that interest other people. I am not interested in sport or politics or scandal. I would say those are the three things that absorb most people. But I am interested in people themselves.

In addition, I have never understood those who fail to understand when I make a distinction, in my parlance, between real people and gay people. They seem to take offence at my phraseology. I once made the distinction at a meeting of a lot of elderly people in The Center on West 13th Street, and a woman, whom I presumed to be a lesbian, rose and angrily announced, "Well, I'm real." And doubtless in her mind she was. To my mind, and again in my parlance, she was not, but I now see that my point of view originates from my transgender predisposition.

As I have said before, the life I've lead has not been one lived in the real world. It has been one long daydream. I wish I had been born a woman and one attracted to men, as I myself once was. That is my definition of real. It's the reality I wished for myself.

Now, I have made it a rule never to recant or apologize in life, so if my phraseology has offended or disadvantaged you or someone you know, all I can do is ask for your forgiveness. Please know that it has never been my intention in this life to hurt another human being.

I'm also aware that my views on gay sex may have also caused hurt in certain circles. To comprehend my views you really have to remember the context in which they were formed. My view of homosexual sex was certainly tainted not only by my experience in London as a rent boy, but by the times during which I was sexually active. When I was young and swanning about the West End of London, men would look at me and smile and I would think, "Oh, this is wonderful. I'm the cat's whiskers." It never occurred to me what I would have to do once I'd won their attention. By the time I realized, from my perspective, it was too late.

With hindsight I would have been happier being celibate in a monastery than in degrading myself before strangers as I did. I thought it would bring people to me and that they would like me and they would be happy, but, of course, they despised me because their interaction with me made them ashamed.

When I was young, no homosexual had an affair with another homosexual because that was just seen as shadow-boxing. It wasn't the real thing. Why? Because more often than not the objects of our affection believed themselves to be heterosexual and there just weren't enough openly gay men to go around. So, you had sex with straight men who despised you. Of course, looking back they weren't straight at all. They were just closeted homosexuals, hence their loathing not only of you but of themselves. Typically one eventually tired of the negativity and lack of happiness and realized that it simply wasn't going to work.

I actually preferred sex with these 'straight' men as it seemed to me to justify my existence. It made me feel like the real woman I was in my head. When I was young, my friends and I all thought that homosexual men were effeminate because those were the only ones we could see. Because all the closeted gay men led quiet, hidden lives, we didn't have them as a reference. Instead we pooled our misery, shared our lipstick, combed each other's hair and talked about our woes. It was a sort of uneasy camaraderie mixed with a lot of bitchiness which in reality was mostly stylized and staged.

Now, of course, I am not attracted to anybody, but when I was young, I was attracted to older, larger more masculine men than me. Men who could take command of the situation. I think what I really wanted was an authority figure and I think I wanted one because it would absolve me of responsibility. I would be able to say, "He drove me to it. He commanded that I do this or that." And I would feel I had been coerced into sinning, which promises all of the associated joys and none of the consequences.

Looking back, I would have liked to have had an affair which nowadays we call a relationship. Only I wouldn't have wanted it to last very long. I don't ever think I wanted an affair to last all night, let alone for weeks or months or years. My dream date would have been a brief affair that was over in under a couple of hours with someone I was never going to see again. I have a sad feeling that's called anonymous sex, but the truth is what it is, I suppose.

Because I am ninety, I can no longer remember when my first sexual experience was, but it probably took place before I was twenty. I went out from my parents' home into the West End and there I trotted about until I had picked up some man or other from whom I tried to get money. This was always very difficult. I didn't really know what I was going to have to do. I think I thought I would be taken to an expensive hotel or apartment, but really I was only going to be taken to a dark doorway in the street whereupon the man would say, "This'll do." Those were the only words of physical love I have ever heard.

It was all so instantaneous. It was with people whose names I never knew. They made sure I didn't know. And I can't remember who was the first or where or why, but the idea behind it all was to justify my existence. I had thought to prove to myself I was really a woman by having sex with a man. I think I only demanded money because that's what my other hooligan friends did.

Since I thought of myself as feminine, the kind of men I wanted to meet were masculine, typically either men in uniform or men of the working class. I believe there exists in homosexual life what I call 'the confection complex.' By it, I mean to describe how many middle and upper class homosexuals want to know boys of lower class because they think of them as more rugged. The confection complex explains why Mr. Forster[9] got to know a policeman and Mr. Ackerley[10] got to know a sailor.

In my case however, I can say simply that I didn't know any wealthy men who thought I needed to be tamed. I knew well-off people, but, of course, when you have nothing, everyone seems to be well-off by comparison. They wouldn't have wanted to know me anyway because the disgrace would have been so great. If you were going to be the friend of a wealthy

---

9 E. M. Forster OM, CH, English novelist, essayist and librettist, 1879-1970
10 J. R. Ackerley, British writer and editor, 1896-1967

man, you had to be his nephew at any moment and I was nobody's nephew.

So, I never really had what you would call 'a love life'. Well, not one that involved other people. I gave up sex at thirty, but continued to masturbate for many years, which is a cozy form of sex in which you are not defiled. You don't run into any danger, you know what you want and it is entirely satisfactory. In this respect, I have enjoyed a long and happy sex life for many years now. It's also a form of sex that sits more easily alongside my daydream.

Had I been born a woman with a vagina, sex would have been quite different. A friend once asked of me, "What's the difference between taking a penis into your mouth and taking it into your vagina?"

I couldn't understand that. Vaginas and penises are both parts of the human body that are never mentioned in polite society. To me, your mouth is your own. You doll it up and poets write about it. It's very different real estate from anything 'down there'.

I don't masturbate at all now because it takes such an effort. In any case, I generally feel ill enough without a hard-on, so why make matters worse? I suppose I masturbated up until the age of sixty, or something like that. After that, it becomes too much of a chore.

No one, of course, needs to be taught how to masturbate. What should happen however, is that the lies surrounding masturbation should be debunked. When I was at school everybody masturbated and everyone was terrified. How much was too much? Was once a day too much? Was once a week too much? Would you go mad? Would you go blind? We would all have been very happy had someone in a position of authority said, "Don't think about it. Masturbating once a week does no harm to anybody."

And it does you no harm, provided you don't try any weird things. Occasionally you hear stories of people strangling or suffocating themselves in the middle of sex. I never understand all that, but I recommend masturbation whole-heartedly.

People always ask me, "When was the last time you had sex?" You can't answer. Because you don't know when it's the last time. You don't get out of bed and think "That's that." and then wipe your hands clean of it. Instead you find that the friends who used to come and see you once every two or three days start to come once every two or three weeks, and then once every two or three months, and then once every two or three years. And then not at all. And you don't think about it again until their name comes up in conversation.

Having given up sex at thirty, imagine my surprise when an African-American man tried to pick me up the other day. I'm now ninety. He was a taxi driver who had just brought me back from the airport. When we arrived outside my house he asked me, "Are you a man or a woman?"

When I told him, "I'm sorry to disappoint you, but I'm not a woman," he asked if I would give him a blowjob. I politely informed him, "I'm afraid I'm too old for any of that sort of thing."

It passed pleasantly and he wasn't angry. He just accepted the fact. I didn't pretend to be shocked or anything like that. That's the only time in America anyone has ever propositioned me.

CHAPTER 2

Influence

I CAN HONESTLY SAY THAT I don't think I've had any influence on anything. Not on modern life. Not on society. The idea that I have had is purely an idea in other people's heads. I have become a self-apparent, elderly foreigner of dubious gender and I don't think anyone's ever really aspired to be that.

More importantly, I am only one person. I'm detached from the world and I never engage in civic activity. Had I started movements and made speeches then perhaps I could claim to have had an influence on the world. I have never done any of that. I have never lived a civic life and I have no political identity or ambitions.

When people claim I have influenced the world, I'm polite. I smile and nod, but I don't really believe it. I can say with certainty however that I haven't allowed the world to influence me, so it seems only fair that the reverse should be the case as well.

I have no regrets for living my life the way I have. I'm very glad that I have lived my life singly because I believe the strain of living with another person would have been so great that I would have broken down. Doubtless, I would have made the mistake of choosing the wrong time to say what I actually thought and that would have been the end of it.

Other people are such a strain. I don't think they realize it, but they nag you all the time. They say, "You're not going to sit around looking like that all day, are you?" Then before you know it you find yourself grooming and beautifying yourself for somebody you already know, which is ridiculous.

However, people who ask if you have any regrets fail to realize that you can only have regrets if you had alternatives. A man who says, "Why did I live with that wretched woman? Why didn't I leave her and marry all those wonderful people over there?" can be sincere in his regret because he believes he genuinely made the wrong choice.

The life I've lived has not been one of missed alternatives. I had only the friends who could put up with the disgrace. I had the jobs from which I was not given the sack. I lived in the digs from which I was not evicted. Looking back I didn't have any alternatives and so therefore I have no regrets.

Perhaps that's not entirely true. I regret having been born, of course, and not having been born a woman. I suppose I have other regrets as well. My biggest regret is that I didn't come to America when I was young enough to accept all the invitations extended to me when I finally did arrive. I could have gone somewhere different every night.

Every day I receive an invitation to the opening of an art show or a gathering of literary people or a poetry reading. These days my body simply won't allow me to attend them all, but had I come here when I was forty then perhaps I might have been able to. I cannot stress enough how much I like New York City.

The only thing I am self-indulgent with is time. I lull about all day doing more or less nothing. I don't pull myself together and do something useful. I don't see any need to. I've never thought, "Oh, I wish I'd learned hang gliding," or something weird like that, and I have no desire to travel to foreign places because I can't speak the local language.

I'm content with the life I have. I live by myself in one room. I never work, I never branch out. I live the life I know will not land me in danger or end in embarrassment or disgrace. That's really my only standard. It probably seems very sinful to other people since I am not doing any good in the world, but neglect can hardly be called sinning. At least I don't do any harm to other people.

As I reach the end of my life, I live very differently than the way I did twenty years ago. The difference is that I now know more people. In England it was very hard for people to know me. They felt they had to conceal the fact. Here in America people want to know me and to be photographed with me. So that's made my life much more pleasant than it was before.

I don't judge myself by that. I don't think, "I must be more wonderful now than I was then." All it means is I know more people who are superficially inclined towards me. My notoriety is what attracts people. They don't bother to think, "Do I really like him?" Nevertheless they're there, they're pleased that they're there and I'm pleased that they're there. People who want to meet me want to know me. In response, I try to know them as well, though I can't ever really know them. There are too many of them. The best I can do is to make myself available to them. I try never to say no to anything.

These days, I'm frequently too ill to attend anything. This makes illness an even sadder event because people don't really believe I'm not well. They still want to meet me and think I've just tired of them and that I'm making excuses. That's a pity because I never tire of anybody.

Without claiming to have achieved anything, I can also say that there remains very little, if not actually nothing, that I want to achieve with the little time I have left. I accept my limitations. I'm in dim cellar movies, which typically take place in this neighborhood, but I have no ambition to be a movie star or anything like that. The image of me that exists in the world is not one that I have deliberately projected.

Ms. Dietrich was the first person I heard use 'image' in its American meaning. She said, "I dress for the image," by which she meant she dressed to please people and probably did since she was a very beautiful and exotic woman.

Nowadays, my appearance is very much part of the way I am. My hair is not long enough or thick enough to cover my head, no matter how I brush or comb it. As such I sort of pile it up on my head. Were the wind to blow, it would point in all directions and become a frightful mess, so I always wear a hat. Now that has become part of my image, but it hasn't been brought about by some grand design.

Of course, I used to dye my hair and wear makeup and nail varnish so I suppose at that time I could have been considered vain. I did care about my appearance when I was younger. I think the difference between being vain and being conceited is that if you are conceited you *think* you're better than other people, whereas if you're vain you know you are.

Previously, vanity described a concern with empty, superficial things. Now it's used to describe a preoccupation with one's appearance. I am concerned with my appearance, but chiefly now for the sake of the world. I think the world wishes to see me looking the way I do because they like you to be the same, to be recognizable. If people feel they can predict you, they feel they own you and if they feel they own you, then they like you.

I've never bothered about my weight. I don't know whether other people have looked at me and thought, "Oh, he's getting fat." or, "He's getting a bit thin." In England, weight is not a problem. It's only a problem in America. Someone said to Mr. Mastroianni[11] when he arrived here from Italy, "You've lost weight."

And he replied, "You Americans are obsessed with the loss of weight."

In fact, the greatest compliment you can pay an American is to say, "You look marvelous. Surely you've lost weight?"

But no, I have never bothered about my weight. I have never been concerned with what I eat and I've never taken any

---

11 Marcello Mastroianni, Italian film actor, 1924-1996

exercise. In short, I have never tried to improve my appearance from within. Which, I think means I'm comfortable with myself. Any alterations I make are applied from and to the outside.

I believe you're called a solipsist if you believe that you are the center of the world and everything else radiates out from that. That's what I do, certainly professionally. I know I am of no importance, but I lapse into thinking that I am. When people tell me how important I am to their lives, I try to relieve the burden and explain that I am entirely superficial. I am something added on, for decoration if you will.

I am important to myself, of course. When you work as a naked civil servant, one of the first things you notice is that art classes are principally made up of housewives. Not long afterwards you realize that all housewives do is talk about their children. They are totally preoccupied with them. I do not have children, so there is no one I am preoccupied with. It's just me.

There are white-collar men who, I think, secretly love the fact that pandemonium ensues when they're not in the office. They like knowing that the cogs and wheels stop turning when they are absent. I'm not part of any organization thank goodness. If I were part of an organization, I would feel bound to take it seriously, which I'm certain would only end in disappointment.

Heartache and heartbreak are what comes from investing your emotional well-being in other people. I have never been heartbroken because I've never cared what other people think of me. Actually, let me rephrase that. I care what *people* think of me, not what *a person* thinks about me. I would only ever be heartbroken if I discovered that the entire public had forgotten about me, which is partly why I left England. Here in America people are nice to me and encourage me to be myself. That's why I live here.

Even in my sixties, during the 1970s, people in England were unkind to me. People would lean out of windows and shout out things like, "You disgusting man!" Now I was old and shabby, yes, but nevertheless that still seems to me to be an exaggerated reaction to someone who was just walking past. But that's what the English are like. If they don't like you, they say so. If they do like you, they keep quiet. Americans are the exact opposite. If they like you, they'll say so and if they don't they'll keep quiet.

During my life I have tried my utmost to deliberately offend no one. I have, in fact, tried my utmost to do nothing of any consequence. I never get bored, however. My sister, towards the end of her life, remembered that when she and our mother would sit either side of our fireplace, busying themselves knitting, reading and writing letters, I, being eight years younger than her, would simply lay on a rug at their feet. Every now and again they would say, "Why don't you do something?"

And I would reply, "Why should I?"

The truth is I like doing nothing. That's why I became a model. It's no good being a model if all the time you're posing, you're thinking, "I could be peeling the carrots if only I were at home. Why haven't they finished? I wonder what time it is?" If you're a model you just stand there and think about nothing except what you're doing.

Of course, the most significant thing I've done in my life was coming to New York. My life changed as a result. Had I lived all of my life in London, I would never have known there was any happiness in the world. When I got here and found that in America everybody is your friend and that living in New York is one big street party, I was so pleased I could have wept for joy.

If I were younger, I would keep in touch with all the people who write to me. I would attend all the first nights, all the gallery openings and all the discotheques to which I am invited. My age has meant I've had to let a great deal of New York life go by, but I still participate in as much of it as I can.

My spies tell me that people have described dining with me as one of the best shows in New York. That is nice, but of course one should never trust reviews. I enjoy meeting people in restaurants because, with luck, they will pay for my meals. Saying this invites the accusation that I am a penny-pincher or mean when it comes to money, but the truth is I have no money because I never work.

I came to America when I was seventy-two, much too old to apply for a job. So, I have never worked nor had any wages. Instead, rather like Ms. Dubois,[12] I have come to rely on the kindness of strangers. They call me up and invite me to dinner. I like to meet them chiefly in neighborhood bars. I don't

---

12 Blanche DuBois, fictional character in Tennessee Williams' play *A Streetcar Named Desire*.

want to go all the way across New York to meet them in some peculiar place which they happen to like. Everyone I know says of every place in which I have met them, "Yes, I remember that, but it's gone off terribly." Actually, it's just the same. It's just that they've been there before and now they want to try somewhere new in case it's better. It's as if they're worried they might be missing out on something if they go to the same place more than once.

Recently I was declared 'The Queen of all Queens'[13] which I found amusing. I've slowly got used to that sort of thing. I've always been the object not of admiration, but of attention. It supports you. It gives your life a kind of meaning and it also changes you. If you are being watched, you behave differently. If you are being listened to, you speak differently. I have no talent at all. I'm simply someone who is accustomed to being observed.

The attention I'm given has never made me feel uncomfortable because I go out and meet it. I always look as if I'm being photographed. I always speak as though I am being recorded. That's the least I can do in return for the attention that is given to me.

I'm often asked whether I consider myself an eccentric, to which I answer, "Not really." The reason I don't consider myself to be an eccentric is because I don't do anything on impulse. I think what makes you eccentric is if people cannot

---

13 By which person, organization or media outlet is not clear, though Sally Potter remarked that being the "Queen of Queens" is one of the reasons she chose Quentin Crisp to play the role of Elizabeth I in *Orlando*, 1992.

calculate what you will do. I simply consider myself to be a logical man. I can explain exactly why I do what I do. Other people may not agree with my logic or may reach a different conclusion, but that does not make me an eccentric. I very seldom find myself saying, "And I can't think what came over me, but then I did this or that or the other."

My life is calculated. People accuse me of being unnatural and affected, but I don't hold that being natural is in any way an advantage. And if people wish to describe my preparedness to speak as being affected then I suppose I am. I can never understand why American politicians seem to lack oratory skills because I would have thought that that was the first thing you need in such a profession. These days though, they simply read the speeches other people write for them. I've never had a speech written for me, though of course the difference is I rarely say anything that matters.

Having become known as a raconteur, commentator or wit (and the truth is I will accept any title or label people choose to give me) I'm asked about such a variety of subjects that I can't possibly have opinions on all of them. So from time to time, I have to manufacture an opinion, which sometimes makes an answer less spectacular than it might otherwise have been. Or sometimes more controversial and more spectacular, in which case it is my duty to stand by what I have said, else I lose my reputation as a source for comment. These days I often feel I am just repeating myself. I hope I die soon before I become too boring.

CHAPTER 3

London and Hooliganism

I'VE ONLY EVER MADE TWO decisions for myself. One was to leave home when I was seventeen. The other was to leave England when I was seventy-two. Both were like falling off a cliff in the dark.

I lived in London from the age of twenty-two to the age of seventy-two. All told, a period of some fifty years. Forty-one of them were lived in a room in Beaufort Street in Chelsea.[14] I must have moved there in 1940 just after World War II had begun. Of course, many Londoners fled the capital for fear of being bombed by the Luftwaffe. I couldn't see the point in evacuating. Faced with the threat of Nazi Germany or the housewives of rural England, I chose to face the Hun and would gladly do so again.

Whether by Hitler's orders or otherwise, my house was never bombed. The rest of Chelsea wasn't so lucky however. The house opposite the one in which I stayed caught fire. A firebomb landed on the roof, burned through and fell onto

---

14 129 Beaufort St, Chelsea, London SW3 6BS, United Kingdom

the floor below. It burned through that too until the whole building was engulfed in flames.

Now that I think about it, I was very lucky that my house survived unscathed. I would have hated to have to move and start all over again. It must be terribly upsetting when all your possessions and your clothes get burned. I would be a madman if I lost everything, which is why I always feel sorry when I see news reports of Americans who have lost their homes in hurricanes and tornadoes and things like that.

I was young when I first came to London and I moved incessantly. Part of this was me finding my feet but it was also a search for people who would put up with me. Back then, everything I possessed could be put into two small suitcases. I think this probably made it too easy for me. As I collected more possessions, I moved less and less.

I've never been a collector of valuables. I don't think I've ever owned anything more valuable than a jeweled ring. I like to live knowing that everything I touch is expendable. I think life is less troublesome that way. In addition, I've never cared what the places I've lived in have looked like.

I remember when I first moved to Pimlico[15] in west London. I knew a man called Gerald who was a puppeteer, and I remember him asking me, "Where do you live?"

And I said, "I live on Denbigh Street."

He then asked me, "What's your room like?"

To which I replied, "It's just a room."

---

15 81 Denbigh St, Pimlico, London SW1V 2EY, United Kingdom

And he said, "Have you done anything with it?"

I was surprised by this and said, "What do you mean?"

"Well," he began, "isn't it full of lace curtains and table-cloths with bobble fringes?"

And I said, "Yes."

Having confirmed his worst fears he looked at me sympathetically and asked, "Can you bear it?"

And I said, "Yes. I adore it."

Despite having since been labeled an 'expert' on style and taste,[16] I have certainly not had a problem living in places with distasteful décor. Besides, I find such places to be considerably cheaper than the alternative.

If I have any wisdom on taste and style, it is because I am personally indifferent to both of them. I remember living in London, for a short time, above a woman who had her own dancing studio. She was a taste addict and it got very tiresome. She would come back from a visit to a friend's house and complain to me that, "The furniture was simply glittering with varnish. Terrible taste." Almost everything that happened to her offended her because her taste was 'so exquisite'. "The crockery was in such bad taste. You could hardly drink out of it." I found both of these observations to be quite absurd.

As for my taste, I suppose I care what I wear, but I think what I wear would be called bad taste by other people. It's showy. You see, good taste is a question of being restrained, I think. At least in England it is. You have to wear dark clothes

---

16 Quentin published *How to Have a Life Style* in 1975 and *Doing It With Style* in 1981

and never wear a diamond tiepin or other things like that. If it's ostentatious, it's in bad taste.

I hope never to go to England again. The very idea exhausts me. I did go last autumn to promote a book called *Resident Alien* which was a bad title because there is a film called *Resident Alien* and there is no connection between the book and the film. The book was originally going to be called *Among Friends* which I considered a good title, but I suppose someone somewhere must have thought they knew better.

While I was there, I wandered through Soho. I took a walk along Old Compton Street, through Soho Square, down Rathbone Place and then Charlotte Street. Everything had changed except the pubs which were decorated in the same way, populated by the same people standing in the same positions drinking the same drinks. I found this to be both comforting and disturbing in equal amounts.

Soho was, of course, my old stomping ground. I may have slept in Chelsea for more than forty years, but during all that time I *lived* in Soho. I would wake up and go to work as a model in whichever art school it was that day. Then, when I had spare time, I would go to Soho to visit my friends.

Soho appealed to me because it was more or less a Mediterranean district run by Italians and Greeks. The Italians, as you well know, invented murder, so someone was always being stabbed or shot, which made it an exciting place to hang around in. It was a bohemian place and you did what you liked, wore what you liked and could generally be yourself.

In Soho there was no prejudice. My friends and I would sit all day long in cafés talking. Conversations tended to be about thought-provoking ideas, serious and nonsensical in equal measure, as opposed to the fishwives' gossip that pervaded establishments elsewhere in London. Chelsea was full of gossip. Gaggles of barren women would meet regularly in venues along the Kings Road and talk maliciously about whoever wasn't there that day.

Fitzrovia was another area where the bohemians went, although there the conversations tended to get more political. I've always tried to avoid politics wherever possible. A lot of the patrons in Fitzrovia were communists. If I say the conversations were philosophical, that makes it sound a bit pompous. It's better if I describe it as talking for talking's sake. It was about ideas and it was wonderful.

When I look back, I don't really miss my cohorts, the other hooligans. The actress Anna Wing[17] was one of them. She ended up becoming rich through playing the part of Lou Beale in the British television series *Eastenders*. Now she lives in Brooklyn and works at the Academy of Music there. She must be about ten years younger than I am which means she's been acting for a very long time.

She telephoned me to tell me she was here and I remember saying in a suitably mournful voice, "I have an enlarged heart."

And she replied nonchalantly, "Oh, I've got one of those."

---

17 Anna Wing, English theatre and television actress, 1914-2013

So, perhaps I'm taking the whole thing too seriously. I would have thought working in Brooklyn was enough to give anyone a heart attack, but somehow she's managing it.

There aren't many hooligans left these days. That's the trouble with living so long, you watch all the people you once knew fall by the wayside. There was a woman called Mrs. Woolf[18] who was the wife of Cecil Woolf in turn the nephew of Virginia Woolf. I don't know what happened to her.

There was a woman called Mable McCallister, an actress who was so difficult that she never got any parts. There were various men. The only famous people were Arnold Wesker[19] who wrote the play called *Chips With Everything,* and the painter Lucian Freud,[20] grandson of the famous Mr. Freud,[21] though he was always rather condescending.

Certain objectionable people existed as well. There was a man called Iron Foot Jack[22] who ran The Caravan Club in the 1930s which was a club of ill repute that was raided often. When I say it was a place of ill repute, I mean that it was a meeting place for homosexuals, which in my time I visited. Although men at The Caravan did nothing more than dance with each other, Jack and a number of the club's patrons were arrested. It was quite a scandal and he ended up

---

18 Jean Moorcroft Wilson, British academic and writer, b. 1941
19 Sir Arnold Wesker, British dramatist, 1932-2016
20 Lucian Freud,, British painter, 1922-2011
21 Sigmund Freud, Austrian neurologist and the founder of psychoanalysis, 1856-1939
22 Jack Neave, Australian nightclub owner, c. 1886- c. 1961

being sentenced to two years in prison, I think, for 'keeping an immoral place'.

The Wheatsheaf on Rathbone Place was a pub where all the bohemians went, the sort of people who wrote books and poems or painted pictures. Really, they were all unsuccessful artists. They wrote books which didn't make any money. They painted pictures which were put in exhibitions but never sold. Basically, they didn't want to work. Consequently they had no money and if they ever came into any money they drank it.

Although the people I'm describing were generally friendly towards me, the safe houses weren't always particularly safe, particularly for me. You see, the English dislike effeminacy and I, of course, was the embodiment the of limp-wristed wistfulness they hated. It wasn't so much that I was homosexual, more that I behaved like a woman. In those days women were very much treated like second class citizens.

Englishmen are always saying, "Oh, you know, she's always asking if I really love her and all that rubbish. She'll fiddle with her appearance and ask me how she looks. It's very annoying." Americans expect their girlfriends to do that. They call their girlfriends 'sugar' and 'honey' and 'baby' and their girlfriends like it and bask in this adoration of their femininity.

Ms. Monroe[23] was an ideal of womanhood because she was so excruciatingly feminine, not only to look at but in every possible way. The English would never have put up with

---

23 Marilyn Monroe, American actress and model, 1926-1962

that. They would have said, "Off with her head!" In England, women have to become pseudo-men to get on. When Mrs. Thatcher[24] ruled England, I admired her enormously because she ruled a country which fundamentally hates her gender. She had to give up being a woman in order to rule, which was a pity. Had she stayed feminine and still ruled, it would have been wonderful.

The most famous of the hooligans was a woman called Nina Hamnett[25] who was described by Walter Sickert,[26] the famous painter, as the greatest woman draftsman of the century. She didn't do anything except drink. You never saw Nina Hamnett eating. I would never have described her as perpetually drunk, but you would always see her slightly tottering as she walked down the street. She was openly bisexual. She committed suicide in the end. I think she saw a play about her and it made fun of her. I think she didn't like that and that's why she killed herself. She threw herself out of the window and impaled herself on the fence below. That takes some nerve. She must have been at least fifty.

The barkeepers in Soho and Fitzrovia were alright but, of course, they were in cahoots with the police. When I got chucked out of the Wheatsheaf, my friends rushed in and asked, "Why have you turned out Mr. Crisp?" and Mr. Redfuss, who I think was the barkeeper at the time, answered, "I don't care what Mr. Crisp does, or what he is, but the police

---

24 Margaret Thatcher, Prime Minister of the United Kingdom, 1925-2013
25 Nina Hamnett, Welsh artist and writer, 1890-1956
26 Walter Sickert, English painter and printmaker, 1860-1942

have been in and they said to me, 'You run a funny place.' And I said, 'Funny?' and they looked at Mr. Crisp and said, 'That kind of funny,' and he told me I'd lose my liquor license if I'm not careful."

I didn't go there again after that.

What happened at The Wheatsheaf wasn't typical of Soho however. I think there were only one or two pubs I wasn't allowed in. It was much easier for me to enter an establishment in Fitzrovia. I wouldn't have attempted to go to a pub in a normal, respectable district. I wouldn't have been allowed in.

I once went into a restaurant and having sat down, the waiter came up to me with a red face and said, "I've been told not to serve you." And so as to not create a spectacle, I got up and left. Not indignantly. They couldn't help it. They just didn't want to lose their license.

I used to go to a tacky café called The French where a lot of my friends used to go. One day I went in and greeted everybody and smiled and a man whose name was, I think, Livingston suddenly turned on me and said, "You like being here, don't you? At least the other people know they should be somewhere else, but you actually enjoy it." He was quite angry.

Although his outburst surprised me, I told him, "I wouldn't come here if I didn't enjoy it." Which I think may have irritated him further.

I left home at the age of twenty-two in 1931 when I moved to London and began living with the terrible man whom I described in *The Naked Civil Servant* using the lines: 'We were not friends. We were not lovers. And soon we were not friends.' But he was good enough to take me in. He had only the dole[27] to live on, so we ended up both living on it. It was a very tough time. I nearly starved. He was two or three months younger than I was and his name was Mr. Anthony Greene. I suppose he could still be alive, but I doubt it so I don't think it matters if I reveal his identity now.

By 1931 I had been to an art school in High Wickham which is where my parents moved to after living in Sutton. Art school taught me nothing that was of any use. Back then the object of all commercial art was to make a drawing look machine made. You used an air-o-graph and instruments like ink pens and compasses. My art school never had any of those things so I didn't know how to use them. As such, even with my art school education, I was unqualified to work in a commercial art department.

I only became an art school model because I was familiar with the work environment and I felt I could do it. I could bear the pain. I could keep still and I could keep quiet. It seemed like the profession I was born to do. I didn't long to display myself. I'm lucky in that the best parts of me are the bits you can typically see: my head, my hands and, if necessary, my feet. The rest of me is a mess, but on the occasions where full nudity was required I disrobed and obliged the class. I've never liked my body.

---

27 An unemployment benefit in the United Kingdom

Students were typically very embarrassed by and contemptuous of art models. If you ever met them in the street, they pretended like they hadn't seen you. They were embarrassed by your existence. Come to think of it, I think they were forbidden when I was first a model to speak to me. They never did, except to say, "Rest. Thank you," or, "Shall we start again? Thank you."

Sometimes they would talk to you so they could inform you what you were doing wrong. Models typically had various reactions to this. I can remember one model, to whom a student complained, "You had your left foot much further back last week."

The model replied, "I know I did, and what a damn fool I was."

Comfort was of the most importance to models, though we did try our best to please the students. It was a thankless task however. You couldn't please any student because all of them, for whatever reason, hated models.

I worried a lot when I was in my twenties though I'm sure I couldn't tell you what I worried about. When I was about twelve or thirteen, I think I realized I was never going to be able to be a real person. I also worried about what I was going to do when I 'grew up'. I remember going with mother down to the station to meet my father who was coming off the train. Alongside him any number of men disembarked all in navy blue suits with briefcases and folded umbrellas. I didn't say anything to my mother but I remember thinking, "I'll never be one of them. I simply don't know how to do it."

I didn't despise them. I just thought it was a world I could never enter.

You see, I have always carried with me a great feeling of inadequacy. I have always felt unable to join the real world. When I went for interviews for office work they would ask me difficult questions like, "Why do you want this job?"

And I would say, "Only to live." Which was the truth, but not the answer they were looking for. I'm not sure I ever worked out what the right answer should have been.

I know other people would boast and say things like, "Well, I wouldn't mind occupying the chair you're in now in twenty-five years time," but I could never have uttered those words.

I knew I would never be the head of an office or department. All the interviews I attended were uncomfortable, which over time made me dread them even more. I didn't really want to make a living and I didn't know *how* to make a living. What I wanted was a job but I knew that if I was given the job of making tea for the rest of the staff, I wouldn't be able to do it. I didn't even know how to make tea. If I had been tasked with sweeping the office, I would have done it badly.

Had I been in America at the age of twenty-three, I would probably have sought out a job in show business since that is the kind of job that everyone in America wants. I'm also aware that I'm showy by nature. I would never have been a star, but perhaps I could have made a living by appearing in crowd scenes in various films and television shows or something like that. I know from what little movie work I've been involved in, that it's something I like. I wouldn't go as far to say that

I'm any good at it, but I can't have been that bad at it because I'm still asked from time to time to do more.

In my view, I remain an outcast, someone who can't fit in, but I mind it less now because I have the answers which an outcast can give. An outsider is not the same as an outcast. An outcast has literally been cast out. He has been reviewed, judged by society and then sent away for some reason. An outsider starts on the outside, or chooses to move to the outside which typically means he's in some way superior, or thinks of himself as superior. That doesn't describe me.

At the age of thirty-two, I moved into the bedsit let to me by Miss Vereker[28] who was among saints. She believed in freedom, love and all that, and all sorts of cranky ideas. She went and protested against battery hens and in support of free-range eggs. Everything that she could care about, she did. Everything that she could be against, say the atom bomb, she was. She even marched to the place in England where the bomb was manufactured. I don't know why.

I suppose I must have been one of her causes, one of the things she cared about because she never turned me out and I lived in that room on Beaufort Street for forty-one years. When I first arrived the rent was two pounds a month, or ten shillings a week. By the time I left I think it had gone up to about six pounds a month, or thirty shillings a week which was still remarkably cheap.

---

28 Landlady of Quentin's bedsit at 129 Beaufort St, Chelsea

Back then, if you wanted to dance with another man it was practically impossible. In the Palais de Dance, girls could dance with one another, but not men. If they tried someone would come and tap them on the shoulder and they would have to get off the dance floor. I don't know why it was more acceptable for women to dance together then, but I think more women went to public dances so they often ended up having to dance together.

Instead there were subscription dances for which men would pay half a crown for a ticket and all meet up in some large room. I remember there was one such room over Woolworth's[29] in Edgeware Road. Some men would wear evening dress while others would be dressed in drag. The events were held in secret, which means of course that everybody knew about it and they were always raided by the police.

When you bought your ticket you were told, "Don't tell anybody. Nobody knows about it," but you knew perfectly well that the police had bought their own tickets for the event as well. Then they would arrive in the middle of the night in their black Marias[30] into which all the people in drag would be bundled in their tiaras and furs.

They would probably spend the night in jail, or what was left of the night since the raids never seemed to take place until about three in the morning. Then they would appear in court the next day, still in drag and looking like they had been pulled through a hedge backwards. The public humiliation

29 A British confectionary, media and sundries retail chain that ceased trading in 2009
30 A slang term for a police van

was considerable. In court they would try and defend themselves by saying, "Well, it was like this, Your Honor…"

But the judge would interrupt them with a cry of, "Six months."

Because your manner alone was considered enough to convict you.

I was never at one of these drag dances, but many of my friends were. I've never danced in the whole of my life, let alone been held in anyone's arms and been twirled about the room. I don't think I would have been very good at it. Consequently though, I've never spent time in jail although I have spent time in a cell in a police station, but only because of the arcane method by which the police would contact the person you sought to come and post your bail.

Back then they asked you to give them the name of somebody, and if he or she didn't answer they would just keep ringing the same number until they eventually got through. I can remember saying, "If they're not in, I can give you a list of alternative people you can call."

But they told me, "We don't want a list. Give us one name."

I wasn't really uncomfortable with the situation since I knew I had done nothing wrong. If I remember correctly I had just been picked up off the street. Ultimately, my friend arrived at about midnight to collect me and I went home and went to bed.

London is a wonderful place. It is only the people that are so awful. When I finally tired of the people, which I think only came after they had tired of me, I decided to leave. That's when I came to America.

These days, I understand *The Naked Civil Servant* is being taught in schools in England. This can only be a good thing. I have come to learn however, that all homosexuals are not alike and of all of them I am probably the least representative, not least because it turns out I am transgender rather than gay. Nevertheless because I and the rest of London thought I was gay at the time, my experience of growing up and living in England is representative of how gay men were treated in the past.

Of course, sex is never mentioned in England. Sex and money are never spoken of in polite society or public forums. I imagine the teachers will focus on my exclusion from society and my reaction to that exclusion. I have no idea how students will react to it. A lot of people over the years have praised my autobiography and claimed it helped them in one shape or form. I hope it has, but I can't help thinking that any formal classroom study of *The Naked Civil Servant* will simply lead to a lot of laughing and giggling. I hope I am proved wrong.

I think D.H. Lawrence[31] said, "It wasn't life that mattered, but watching it being lived." I would say it wasn't watching life being lived that mattered, but saying what you saw because you convert history to your own use by writing about it.

Writing *The Naked Civil Servant* changed my life because it brought me fame and enabled me to move to America on my own terms. Over the years, many people have thanked me for writing the book because it helped them to come out to

---

31 David Herbert Lawrence, English novelist, poet, playwright, 1885-1930

friends or come to terms with their own sexuality. That was not my reason for writing it but any positive effect my writing has had on the happiness of others is to be welcomed.

When *The Naked Civil Servant* was first published, *The Times Literary Supplement* said it was quite an interesting book, but that it was "...a pity it was written in such a jaunty style." As far as I'm concerned, the jaunty style was the only thing which made it acceptable. But I have to admit it *was* written in a jaunty style. Would it have been better if it had been written straight? I don't think it would because mine was such a trivial life.

I'm not offended by criticism. It would take a lot to offend me. I suppose if people accused me of being obsessed with my sexuality which I have tried not to be obsessed with, then I would be offended. But I am obsessed with appearing in public as more like myself than nature has made me, so I suppose I have to put up with that.

I don't think I dress like a woman but I accept that I look like a woman to some people. A lady once wrote to me and said she had seen the video that Sting[32] made for the song *An Englishman in New York* in which I appear. In her letter the lady wrote, "I had thought you were a woman, so I didn't understand why you were in the video or why the song Sting had written was about you." I can understand her confusion though I don't see it myself. I don't think she meant any

---

32 Gordon Sumner, popularly known as Sting, English musician, singer, songwriter, and actor, b. 1951

offence by what she wrote and I wouldn't have been offended even if she had.

I think one's notion of self should begin with an acceptance of your faults. You cannot live a life in which you always think it's other people who are wrong. You can't go around complaining, "They don't understand me. I'm not really like that at all." You have to think, "Am I like how people say I am?" And then you have to either alter it or to go with it according to what you judge to be the wisest thing. You can't just push criticism aside. I think you have to weigh it up and consider the possibility that it could be right.

I abandoned England for New York and advise everyone that if they want to be happy they should come to America. Most English people do not want to be happy. In fact they hold happiness in some contempt. I remember a friend of mine saw a play by Mr. Greene[33] in which the heroine said, "I only wanted to be happy." To which my friend reacted, "What a contemptible idea. Who's happy? People are happy absolutely for only a few moments and even then they don't know it." She wasn't crying when she said that and I think it's a terrible thing to have said. I mean what is the point of living if you don't want to be happy?

Happiness is written into the Constitution of America whereas in England it would be considered to be a frivolous objective. "You ought to have something serious. So grow up. Keep a stiff upper lip. No happiness." I don't know why the

---

33 Henry Graham Greene, English novelist, 1904-1991

English don't want happiness. When I was young and knew nothing else, I thought, "There isn't any happiness and we can't expect it." The extraordinary thing is that in London where no one is happy, there are no protests. America is a place where people can be happy yet there is a protest every day. In America, only the black people aren't happy and that, of course, I understand. For as wonderful as America is, the truth is it will never recover from slavery.

CHAPTER 4

My Life in New York

As soon as I arrived in America in the glorious city of New York, I set out to get myself a green card so that I could live here permanently. Having secured the appropriate documentation, a room, not too dissimilar from the one I had left behind in Chelsea, was found for me on the Lower East Side. When I saw it, I declared triumphantly, "I'll live here." though I was later shocked that the room cost more than $200 a month.

In Manhattan however, there are studios twice the size of my room with a cupboard in one corner with a cooker in it and a cupboard in another corner with a shower in it, that are $1200 a month. Nevertheless, $200 a month was more than I was used to paying back in England. That aside, I have to say that life in America was made very easy for me from the very beginning. I have always been a willing victim of fate and this has led me to what some would call fame, which in turn brought me to America. It's as if my daydreaming finally paid off.

I was sitting in a restaurant on Second Avenue the other day in the window since that is where the owner of the restaurant wanted me to sit, and as people went by they saw me and waved. Naturally, I waved back to them. Then someone sitting at a table near to me asked, "You seem to be famous. Why?"

To which I replied, "I haven't the faintest idea."

I'm aware that I am what might be called a one-trick pony. This I accept without argument. This is why, though I like my friends, I'm mad about strangers because, of course, they haven't 'heard it all before'. It's one thing for you to be halfway through a long story and think to yourself, "I've said all this before." It's something else however, when you look around you and find that the lips of your audience are moving in time with yours. Not only have they heard the story before, they know it verbatim. Somehow people don't mind.

I suppose there's no such thing as being too predictable. In all the English music halls, the comedians had catch phrases for which they were well known. And if they ever failed to mention their catchphrase in the course of their act, the audience would say it for them. As I said earlier, if audiences can predict you, they feel they own you and start to like you. In America however, it's harder to tell if people like you because they are all so kind. Certainly I am under the illusion that Americans like me. I certainly like them.

Unlike the average American however, I never go on holiday or vacation as they call it. I have never felt the need because my life has been one long holiday. Nevertheless, I try not to be unsympathetic to people who long for the weekend to be free of the office or factory in which they have to work. I take no notice of Christmas and Easter and all those things because they're just the same for me. And when I go to visit places, I am not really a traveler because I don't go to see, I go to be seen. So a lot of places tend to look the same to me.

During my years here in America, I've been to a great number of places. One of the places I liked visiting was Key West in Florida which seems altogether to be a holiday island. Nobody seems to work in Key West. It's full with guest houses, piano bars and restaurants. The whole island seems to me to be a shrine to Mr. Hemingway.[34] In every bar there's a life-sized picture of him that says "Hemingway drank here" "Hemingway ate here" "Hemingway wrote here" or "Hemingway fought here." They ought to rename the whole place Hemingway Island. It's a very nostalgic place.

I'm not a great one for nostalgia. I try to live in the continuous present. I do think about the past. Everybody does. But I don't think, "If only I lived there. If only if I had black hair. If only I had those people around me." I like what I have. Someone in England once described me as having 'a disgusting zest for life.' I don't think I do, but I am very content and that seems to be annoying to some people and I never know why.

I lived in Los Angeles for three months, which as you know is New York lying down, but the trouble with Los Angeles is there aren't any people. When you wake up in your hotel on the first morning of your stay and you look out the window,

---

34 Ernest Hemingway, American novelist and journalist, 1899-1961

you wonder what's happened. Has there been an earthquake? Where are all the people because the streets are empty. The answer is, of course, that they're in their cars in traffic jams on the city's various freeways. This means you feel a bit lonely wandering around on foot. In spite of the lack of people on street corners however, I have to say I did like Los Angeles.

I suspect I have been to places in America that I haven't liked but I can't really remember them. I know I've been in places where nothing I could do could entertain the people who had gathered to see me. I was once taken to a terrible place called the Pyramid Club and I thought to myself, "What am I going to do? What am I going to say? These weird people probably expect me to do something bizarre." I decided I had better get out of there as soon as I could, which is exactly what I did.

I can honestly say I haven't been in any danger in America not even here on East Third Street, which makes it altogether different from my early experiences in England. I'm convinced that New Yorkers try to frighten you with stories of New York. They're always saying, "You shouldn't go down there," or "That's a bad street." Well, I've wondered all over the Lower East Side, from which you can get no lower, until midnight and I've never had anything happen to me. I've never had things thrown at me, or been shouted at, or been chased about the place, or anything. I feel thoroughly at home here, which is a first.

I was once on a bus going up Third Avenue when, very discretely, a man squatted down beside me and got me to sign my name on a piece of paper. Then, just as discretely, he went back to his seat. Just then, the woman opposite me said, "Well, who are you then?"

And I asked, "Who indeed?"

She looked puzzled and said, "I thought he was asking for your autograph."

To which I replied, "He was."

Confused, she continued, "Well, why?"

To which I answered, "You must ask him."

By this time the autograph hunter was sitting with his face in his hands and everyone else on the bus was laughing. Finally she turned to the rest of the bus, who she thought must know who I was, and exclaimed, "Who the hell is he?" And everyone roared with laughter.

As I got off the bus, I passed the poor woman and said, "I'm sorry, I wasn't anybody." At which point even the driver of the bus laughed. It could only happen in America.

My preferred methods of travelling are to walk, to go by bus or to go by taxi, but I have been on New York City's subway. My first time on the subway happened when I was with my friend Mr. Ward[35] when we were catching a train at Penn Station bound for Providence, Rhode Island. We had taken a taxi up 8th Avenue and had got stuck in traffic. Later we realized we could go no further than 14th Street anyway because 8th Avenue was closed for a street festival. By then we only had fifteen minutes to make the train. It was a frightful rush but we managed to make the train by taking the subway the

---

35 Phillip Ward, Quentin's best friend, b. 1956

remaining distance. I have to admit I find New York's subway a little gloomy. I much prefer to stay above ground but from time to time I am forced to take the subway because all other ways of getting there are impracticable.

One time, I was on the subway going to Brooklyn and I had to stand because there was no room for me to sit. Imagine my surprise upon realizing I was the tallest person in the carriage. Brooklynese people must be a particularly short race of people. Are they Jewish? Are they Italian? That I didn't notice. The carriage was so crowded that day you didn't have to hold on to anything to remain standing even as the train lurched from side to side. You just leaned upon the people next to you and if you fell into someone particularly badly you simply said, "Oh, I'm so sorry."

My time in America has been happier than any other in my lifetime. Partly this is because people are my only pastime and in Manhattan there are always plenty of people. While I was waiting on the street for a taxi today, two separate people called out, "Hello, Mr. Crisp."

And, of course, I said hello back.

"You don't know me," they each continued in one way or another, "I just wanted to say hello." Then they walked on.

It was nice, but why was it nice? I thought about it and I realized I feel comforted to be with people who know who I am and who are generally pleased with my existence. That makes *me* pleased.

I don't think I'm a hedonist however. A hedonist lives for pleasure, I do not. I do things to be justified. Then again, I suppose I hold that the purpose of life is to be happy, so perhaps I am a hedonist? I do take pleasure in living in the present. I think that's how animals live. They're at one with their surroundings.

Had I grown up in America, my outlook and my way of being would doubtless have been quite different. It would have been much less shrill than it is, especially if I had been born in a big city like New York, San Francisco, Los Angeles or Chicago. Had I been born here, I don't think I would have needed to behave in such a defiant way as I did in England. I was always swimming against the tide over there.

Lately, it has been my speaking engagements with Mr. Lago[36] that have taken me around America and further afield. By further afield, I am mainly referring to Canada where I will be visiting later this year. The first time I visited Toronto, I flew in from England and stayed at the Toronto Hotel. It was only while pondering the meaning of Nova Scotia that I came to the realization that the Scots were the ones who discovered Canada. Doubtless, closely followed by the French.

Mr. Lago and his friend Mr. Snell[37] arrange for me to go to various places and work in tiny, arty theaters, and tell the inhabitants there how to be happy. At the end of the show I am found in another room sitting at a table, pen in hand, ready to sign the books that the audience can buy in the theater's foyer.

---

36 Charles Lago, Quentin's manager from 1995 and founder of Authors on Tour
37 Charles "Chip" Snell, an associate of Charles Lago

These tours send me to places like San Francisco, Atlanta, Philadelphia and Baltimore, to name just a few. The last time I went to Baltimore it was burning hot. I'm sufficiently ignorant of American geography that I didn't even know Baltimore has a seacoast and a harbor. I have also been to Portland and San Francisco, the latter of which was the only town in the world where I have had entirely bad notices. Having said that, the last time I went they were nice to me, so perhaps they are slowly warming to me.

Mr. Lago makes it all so very easy for me. He even sends me an airline ticket. I have to confess I have never bought an airline ticket in my life. Air travel really is easier than any other form. You can hardly do it wrong. I have never yet got on to a plane, sat down and made myself comfortable and heard the stewardesses say, "Welcome to Flight 123 to Los Angeles," and thought, "Oh, I thought I'm meant to be going to Atlanta," and rushed off the plane. So far I've always done it right.

Sometimes someone comes and says, "You're in the wrong seat, Mr. Crisp." And they take my luggage and move me into the First Class cabin, usually because First Class is almost empty. When that happens it's nice because there's so much more room. Recently I was given a bottle of wine by the cabin crew, which I suppose was going spare. The woman sitting next to me asked, "Are you somebody special that we should know about?"

I replied, "I don't think so. Only to the staff on this airplane."

These days I'm much better at making connections because I'm usually sat in a wheelchair and I'm wheeled to wherever it is I have to go which often is a very long way. It's necessary because at my age I can hardly walk at all with my luggage. I don't rely on my fame, you understand. I rely on my helplessness. They can see that I am an old man and that I can't move fast and are generous enough to help me on my way.

John F. Kennedy airport is absolutely hell to get out of. It really is a miserable airport. I find La Guardia much easier. It's reportedly the most dangerous airport in the world, but if you happen to land safely, it's easy enough to get into town from. Apparently, they've been meaning to lengthen the airstrip by 400 yards for six years now, but haven't yet gotten around to doing it. So planes are always either arriving too low and catching their undercarriage on the edge of airstrip, or coming in too steeply so that they can't come to a stop after landing and run on into the river. I suppose when a plane full of people die in the river they'll eventually do it.

I've never been to Mexico or any other country where I don't speak the language. Since my performance is entirely speech, and since what I say has to be translated from English into American before it can be translated into any other language, it's never really crossed my mind to go to Mexico.

I was once invited to go to Costa Rica, but of course I speak no Spanish. The man who invited me said it didn't matter, but I couldn't help but think it would. People always say I'm capable of learning a foreign language, but I think I'm too old for learning now. Besides, you have to know a language very well before you can tell jokes in it. I'm not sure jokes even exist in French. I am willing to believe they might in Spanish.

CHAPTER 5

My Family

SINCE I AM LEAVING THIS world without what I believe people refer to as a 'significant other', and since I have borne no children, you might very well think that the great, though assumed, name of Crisp will fade to dust at the same time I do. You would be mistaken, however. For although in the past I gave the impression that I was raised as an only child, that was most definitely not the case.

In this chapter I would like to introduce you to my family so that you can rest more easily knowing that what Mr. Watson[38] and Mr. Crick[39] would call my DNA is still splashing gaily around the planet's gene pool. Let me start with my chief enabler, my mother.

My mother was very beautiful and always more stylishly dressed than any of our neighbors. She played bridge and did all the things she felt she *should* do. Ladies would come to the

---

38 James Dewey Watson, American molecular biologist and geneticist, co-discoverer of the structure of DNA, b. 1928

39 Francis Harry Compton Crick, British molecular biologist and biophysicist, co-discoverer of the structure of DNA, 1916-2004

house and play bridge with her in the afternoons, but would all leave for their respective homes in time to greet their husbands home from work.

When I look back, I realize my mother was, of course, invincibly snobbish. Previously she had been a nursery governess and in this capacity had experienced life in the houses of the rich. This had gone to her head. I believe she wanted to re-create that atmosphere in our small house on a side street in Sutton and, looking back, probably went to absurd lengths to do so.

We were a small family with very little money, but nevertheless we had a maid in a black uniform with a starched cap and apron who served meals and stood behind us in the dining room while we ate. This, of course, was nonsensical.

The failure of my parents' ill-conceived marriage was plain: my mother was extravagant and my father was penniless. It's not a good combination. The fault wasn't solely my mother's though because my father never told her how much he earned. She just knew he was a lawyer and assumed they were set for life. She didn't much like living in Sutton and must have said to him, "Why can't we move to a bigger house in the country?" He probably replied that they couldn't afford it, which doubtless she wouldn't have believed. It's true my father was a lawyer, but unfortunately for my mother he was a bad one.

I now know for a fact that he was penniless because my mother's sister told me that bailiffs once visited my parents' earlier house in Carshalton, the town in which they lived before I was born. Back then they only had a son and a daughter. So quite what they were thinking when they were penniless and had two extra children, I can't imagine. I think that's why my father hated me so. I was another expense he could ill afford.

In spite of the fact we couldn't afford them, I loved the servants who worked for us, principally because they paid attention to me and praised me. I could dance before them and act for them and tell them long, elaborate stories. They watched and listened, not because I was necessarily any good, but because it meant they could take a break from dusting the stairs or whatever else it was they were doing. My mother would have preferred that they went on sweeping the stairs. She firmly believed in the separation of the classes.

Growing up then, I was actually one of four children. I had two brothers and a sister. While parents sometimes talk of the joy brought to them by their offspring, I can't help but think we were a terrible burden on my mother. My sister might have been of some use to her, but my brothers and I all went on in the way young Englishmen do. We got up and shouted, "Mother. Where are my socks?" And she would say, "Where they always are. In the sock drawer." And, of course, we couldn't find them, so she would have to come upstairs and find a pair of socks and give them to us. We never did anything for ourselves. We must have worn her ragged. I think that's why she insisted on a maid.

As a child, my parents celebrated my birthday, which is on Christmas Day, by giving me two presents. I think only the immediate family gave me two presents. Strangers and other people simply gave me one 'combined' present for Christmas and my birthday, an act that would always make me feel short-changed. My mother would wrap up my presents and write tags that said 'Merry Christmas' or 'Happy Birthday' which was her way of acknowledging the difference.

I am told that in America for your birthday you get spanked the number of your birthday years. So I imagine Americans must dread having birthdays. Nothing like that ever happened to me. In fact, though my childhood was miserable, I was never ill-treated in any way. I have to emphasize that or risk you thinking my parents were ogres. They weren't. They just struggled to cope with *me*.

I can remember one day when we were all sitting down to a meal. My mother was cutting up the dog's food when suddenly she burst into tears. We were horrified. My eldest brother got up from the table and fetched her a glass of water after which she was alright. Then, being English, we all went on as though nothing had happened. At the time I thought, "Why did she do that?" But, of course, she was just really worn out.

When I was young, my mother mattered most in my life. She was always there, she tried to understand me and would, alternately, protect me from the world and try and adapt me to it. She never really succeeded at either.

I remember her once sending me to a fancy dress party dressed as a girl. She must have understood that was how I wanted to go and given in. I must have been about seven or eight at the time. I also remember her permitting me to appear in a production of *A Midsummer Night's Dream*[40] dressed as a fairy. To my mind, she knew my desire was to triumph as a woman.

As I grew older, I think she regretted these decisions. Her new tactic was instead to try to toughen me up so that I could live in the 'real world'. She wasn't concerned at all with what those of faith might consider 'my sin'. No, she was concerned with my unemployability. What was I going to do to earn a living?

Of course when I reached adulthood, I reached the conclusion that there was really nothing I *could* do to earn a living. So I wrote and illustrated books, I taught tap dancing and I was a model for various art schools. I had no talent for any of those things, but what else could I do? I did them well enough to sustain myself and somehow I survived. At the peak of my working life I think I earned four pounds a week. Whenever I spoke with my mother, up until the day she died, she would always say the same thing. It might have even been the last thing she ever said to me, "Are you *still* out of work?"

By contrast, I don't ever remember chatting with my father. My father seldom, if ever, spoke. He would say things and you would reply, but it wasn't what you could call a conversation. He never told you what his thoughts were about anything. My mother made fun of him in a mild way and, I suppose, we learned to do the same.

My father was a red-haired, nearly bald, very plain man of medium height and medium build. If you saw him in a crowd

---

40 *A Midsummer Night's Dream* by William Shakespeare

going to work, he would have looked just like everyone else. My father never talked to my mother. I never remember a discussion between them or an exchange of jokes or anything that you might call human. He would address or remark to her and she would reply. That was it. Although I was, naturally, a disappointment to my father, he went on as though nothing unpleasant had happened and disregarded me.

I can remember not being able to go back to school because my father wouldn't pay my school fees. It was what Americans would call a private school, but which the English erroneously refer to as a public school. All the boys went on to be doctors and lawyers. I had earned a small scholarship which made the fees slightly less than they otherwise would have been, but I'm sure my father thought, "Why should I pay for this wretched rat to go to school?"

When I *was* at school, I was taught subjects which even at the time, I thought were of questionable use. For example, I knew the names of all the currents in the Pacific Ocean. I've never used the information. I think they simply taught you things to stimulate your capacity to learn.

Classes typically consisted of about twenty-five boys. Some masters could keep the class quiet while others were never able to assert control. I should think they very quietly got the sack in the end. Some masters were quite liked, but mostly you didn't like them and they didn't seem to like you.

Everything I did at school caused comment. Even the boys who liked me would ask, "Do you have to stand like that? Put your hands down." They tried teaching me to be a schoolboy, but I never learned. It wasn't natural to me and I suffered as a result. Had I gone to a girls' school, I wouldn't have suffered at all. That would have been wonderful.

But I digress.

I never explicitly mentioned my homosexuality to my mother and she never mentioned it to me. Nevertheless is was apparent to her and everyone else in our family. I know my mother would have done anything to have avoided the 'terrible trouble' that was me: the anger of my father; the hatred of my brothers and my sister; and all the weeping and wailing that went on simply because I was gay.

Although my mother and father hated each other, they never raised their voices at one another. Moreover, in spite of her predicament, I don't think my mother wished her life were vastly different from what it was. Towards the end of her life with my father having died many years previous, my mother admitted, "I don't know why I married your father. I never loved him. In fact, I hated him."

To which I replied, "We all hated him, Mother. You just hated him enough to marry him."

My mother seemed to like and agree with this explanation, that her marrying him was just some elaborate form of revenge for wrongdoing early in their courtship.

In contrast to me, both of my brothers went on to have long, successful careers. One of them worked as an accountant for a large petroleum company and travelled for a time to China on business. The other worked for a telecommunications company in South America for thirty years and ended up living in Chile.

Now, while it may be true that artists adopt flamboyant appearances, it's also true that people who 'just look funny' get stuck in the arts and that's principally what happened to me. I looked then much as I look now, though perhaps not as exaggerated as I now look. My hair was probably dyed red and was long by the standards of the day. Nowadays, when your hair can be down to your waist, it isn't considered long, but in those days no decent man had any hair showing lower than his hat.

The attitude towards gay people has also changed from when I was young. People have come to accept them. Back then, they didn't really think they existed. They thought they were sort of very far-fetched people who adopted a homosexual lifestyle in order to attract attention. My sister used to say of me, "Oh, he just wants to be different." I didn't. I wanted to be the same. I just *happened* to be different.

These days I'm less worried by what is said of me or to me or how I'm treated and I'm less shrill when speaking about homosexuality. My increased age is entirely the cause of this. Now that I'm older, people know my sex life is non-existent. Consequently, I'm no 'danger' to anyone. This has enabled me to embrace 'the profession of being' in my twilight years, the only profession to which I have ever really been suited.

My sister succeeded in marrying a clergyman, which I now realize was something she had always longed to do, though not, I don't think, for reasons of faith. When we lived in Sutton, we used to make fun of her and say she was in love with the local vicar because on Sunday mornings she would go down to the local church and arrange the flowers and clean the brass.

Her ambition to enter parochial life was not helped by her lack of physical beauty. My sister was not at all pretty. Though one of my brothers had, like her, inherited red hair from my father, both of my brothers were fairly good-looking. My hair, like my other brother's, was the color of a mouse. In spite of this disadvantage however, my sister managed to bag her vicar and the two of them went to live in a country parish in Devonshire.

To my mind my parents were what I would call Anglo-Catholics, which is Catholicism mixed with water. My parents went to church and dragged us with them, but even as a child I knew it was more of a social occasion than an act of worship. My parents made sure we were all dressed up before we went. Once at church, I would sit there silently waiting for the service to end. We never talked about God. Had I ever said to my parents, "Do you believe in God?" I'm sure they would have been shocked.

Undoubtedly they would have replied, "Of course we do."

But really the whole thing seemed to me to be a show.

These days religion has no hold over me at all. When I was young, I did believe in God and I thought he might jump out from a tree at any moment and chastise me for whatever it was I was doing at the time. So, I was haunted by the idea of this watchful but unsympathetic god. By the time I was fourteen however, I had more or less given up on the whole idea.

I think I prayed as a child. I think I knelt down beside my bed and put my hands together and said, "God bless Mother and Father," and so on. I don't think I really believed in what I was doing. I think I did it because I believed my parents would be shocked if I didn't. It wasn't because God might be angry with me.

Telling you all about my family is important because when I was young my family was almost all the people that I knew well. We didn't really have another family near at hand into whose house we ran in and out of. Our family was quite separate from the others that lived around us, not that we were a close knit family by any means. I think that's the shame of suburban life in England. You live in your house and you occasionally invite people in, but you put on a show for them when they do. You want them to see you at your best. You never show them the way it really is.

When my father died, my mother went to live with my sister and her clergyman. No one thought this was a good idea, but where else could she live? Although my sister claimed she never had a row with her, I know my mother complained about everything and, of course, my sister's life was ruined by her presence.

She could never go away for more than four hours at a time without going back to deal with my mother. My mother was more or less confined to her bed because of rheumatism and if she ever left she had to be lifted out and put into a wheelchair. It was a terrible penance, both for her, my sister and my brother-in-law, but they managed and that's how their lives passed. It would have been pure hell had Mother moved in with me, but by that time I had left home and was living in London. Then, of course, the war came so she wouldn't have been able to live with me anyway.

Had my mother not complained about everything in life, she would not have been herself. By the time she died, her hands were frozen in the position for holding canasta cards, much like my own left hand is now. I do not miss my mother because I have now lived without her for so long. She was buried in the churchyard of my brother-in-law's parish. My father was buried in the same place. He died when I was only twenty-two.

Now, of course, my immediate family are all dead: my mother, father, sister and my two brothers. Although I was the youngest child of my mother's brood, I have also lived the longest. It's almost as if You-Know-Who has blessed me with longevity to make up for the suffering of my early life. Though of course he didn't bless any of them with long life for having to suffer me.

Is my bloodline about to run out then? Well, yes and no. I may not have multiplied as our supposed creator instructed, but all three of my siblings did. The result is that I now have three nieces whose attitudes towards my notoriety are vastly different from those of my brothers and sister. Whereas my siblings were embarrassed, my nieces, my great-nephews and great-niece regard the whole thing as a bit of a joke.

When I went to Cheltenham, a very respectable country town in Gloucestershire, to visit my English niece, to my surprise she had invited all of her neighbors in and thrown a bit of a surprise party in my honor. As we entered her living room, her first with me following behind, she announced, "This, believe it or not, is my uncle." and everyone roared with laughter and smiled, which was nice.

I'm lucky to now find myself in a family in which there are no terrible feuds. Or at least none that I am aware of. Others are always recounting stories that begin, "My Aunt Esmeralda shut herself in a room for thirty years and wouldn't speak to anybody," but none of that has ever happened to me. My nieces all get on with one another. Mind you, that could be because they don't see awfully much of each other. Instead of living in each other's pockets, they write to each other from their respective corners of the world. Maybe that's the secret.

CHAPTER 6

Being a Tramp

ALTHOUGH THESE DAYS MY LEGS can barely carry me to the end of the street, when I was young I walked everywhere. In fact, I once walked from Pentonville, north London, all the way to Berwick, Scotland, in ten days covering a distance of around three hundred and fifty miles. Looking back, I believe this was a formative event that helped shape my attitude toward the outside world. Which is why I thought I would include it in this book.

It was the beginning of World War II and I must have been about thirty-one or thirty-two years old. A woman who lived in the same house as me in Chelsea had gotten a job in the Women's Land Army, an organization peculiar to England that sought to make use of female labor at home while the country's men went off to fight the Germans.

Women that got jobs in the Land Army typically ended up working on farms growing, I suppose, food that the soldiers and the rest of the wartime nation could eat. My friend had secured a job on a farm in Scotland, but had then complained to me, "I don't want to take a train there, but I don't want to walk there either. Were I to walk, I would surely be raped by a battalion of Canadian soldiers in a field."

Reassuringly I promised I would come with her to protect her. "Fear not," I said, "I will accompany you so that, should we come across a battalion of Canadian soldiers in a field, they will have to rape both of us."

My friend agreed, so the two of us walked heel and toe from dawn until dusk for ten days without ever stopping, apart from sleeping. When we slept we stayed in people's barns and slept on the ground or straw. We never washed since we had no access to running water. We effectively became tramps which is a Britishism that translates into American as 'hobos'. It was an eye-opening experience.

We walked up the Great North Road forever, from pretty much the beginning until the very end. We walked about thirty-five miles a day, each of us carrying our packs on our backs. We passed through Hatfield, Stevenage, Huntingdon, Peterborough, Grantham and Retford before we arrived in Doncaster.

We got a lift from a lorry driver in Doncaster who took us about seventy miles through Yorkshire to Darlington. Our feet were blistered and aching by this time. We both rode up in the front with him. I can't remember what he looked like, but I can remember him being keen that we talk to him. Lorry drivers seem to take in hitchhikers because they keep them awake. When you accept a lift with a lorry driver he says, "Speak to me." and you talk to keep him awake because if you don't and he falls asleep, the lorry flies off the road and everyone inside dies.

It seems that merchants are sufficiently mean that they give lorry drivers the maximum amount of goods to take and the minimum amount of petrol, gasoline in American, and time with which to deliver it. I suppose it's cheaper, but if you put smaller loads on lorries and gave them longer to make the journey, there would be no accidents at all. I don't suppose that's ever going to happen though. Anyway, the current system works well for hitching a lift.

Aside from lorry drivers however, when you're a tramp no one notices you. Or perhaps it's more accurate to say that while people notice you, they ignore you. By the time we reached Newcastle, we stopped and sat on the edge of a public fountain to eat a chocolate bar. Had we done that as real people and not in disguise as two tramps, people or the police would have come up and said harsh words to us. We would have been accused of loitering or of sitting where we should not have done. But because we were tramps, we were exempted. It was as if we were part of the scenery.

People would look at us, but wouldn't really see us because they would avert their eyes or turn their heads to not see you. It's similar to what Americans do when they pass the homeless on the street here in New York City. Our clothes were not particularly tattered, but they were, of course, very worn and very dirty because we slept in them. We never changed our clothes and I have to say, I very much enjoyed the anonymity my new uniform gave me.

Obviously, I remember being very, very tired. The walking sapped the energy from me. It meant I had no energy for talking. I can't say my friend and I solved the world's problems between us on the way up to Scotland. All we seemed to have energy for was walking. As we neared the end, putting one foot in front of the other was the only movement I could make. I couldn't lift my leg up or move sideways and my ankles were the size of my knees.

My weariness and grime made me at one with the other tramps. I met quite a few along the way and they recognized me as one of them. They didn't stop and talk to you. They simply hailed you and then walked on. They would say, "Hi." Then they would nod and you would reply and nod back.

At Berwick, I came back by train. My friend went on another twenty miles or so to the farm where she was to work. Having walked with her over such a long distance I suppose I could have gone with her all the way to the farm. She insisted there was no need however and, had I gone further, I would have had to double back to get to the station and a train that would take me to London. Perhaps she thought her appearance was enough to deter would-be rapists over the last twenty miles now that she looked and smelled like a vagabond.

Now that I think about it, I don't think we met any soldiers on our trek. We came into contact with police occasionally who assumed we had failed to register for military service, but we had papers saying each of us were incapable of being graded. In my case for being homosexual. So, we got away with it and they let us be.

When I returned to London I made a point of going to see people, still covered with dirt and not having shaved for ten days. My friends recoiled and screamed and ran away at the sight of me, which was great fun.

That's the only time I've ever been voluntarily out of London on foot. There were times I went to schools around London to pose and then, of course, I didn't walk because I knew I would have to stand when I got there. Instead, I took a local train from stations like Victoria and Clapham Junction to go to places in Kent and the various other 'home counties'. Otherwise, I always lived my life in England in London and as you know, Dr. Johnson[41] said, "He who tires of London, tires of life."

I include the story of my time as a tramp here because I think it was formative. These days, all of the clothes I wear are given to me. I never buy clothes myself. I actually never shop. It would be nice to think that the clothes that are given to me are new, but I know they are not. Many are what in England would be called secondhand. As such, some of them can appear worn while others slightly misfit me. If you observe this and take into consideration the state of my room, for as I have famously stated before, I never dust, and the fact that these days I am seldom able to wash properly, you may well agree with me that the time I spent as a tramp in my early life has prepared me for my life in old age.

When giving advice on style to others, I emphasize that I am not asking them to look as I do, merely to ask themselves the same questions that I have. Their conclusions may well be different from the ones that I reached. Nevertheless, I am

---

41 Samuel Johnson, English writer, poet, biographer, editor and lexicographer, 1709-1784

free to give this advice because I have freed myself from the constraints that others buckle under. This gives me time to observe. This means that whether or not I have good or bad taste myself, I am able to discern it, good and bad, in others.

My aversion to shopping comes from never really having worked and the fact that frugality has become a habit for me over the years. My dislike of shopping is surprising however, when you remember that I should have been born a woman. Had I been, I wonder if I would have been a very good woman. When it comes to buying things, the differences between the sexes is that men shop whereas women go shopping. I've never heard a man say, "I went out to buy a shirt. I didn't see one, but I saw this very beautiful mackintosh so I bought it instead." Women do it all the time. They come back with just the things they don't want because they couldn't find the things they did want.

You'll never see me in 'the best shops'. It would be a waste of time. A woman who came to photograph my room commented on the various plastic bags that were lying around. One of them was from Henri Bendel, which had been given to me by a man who worked at Henri Bendel when he had brought some things for me. Another one was from Lord & Taylor, but had been similarly presented to me. The lady photographer beamed as she began snapping away "Oh. I see you shop at all the best shops." To her, she had paid me a compliment. For me, I took what she said to be insulting.

People who shop in 'the best shops' are the people who swan about from one department to another talking loudly and giving the assistants hell. I try to dislike no one, but I couldn't dislike them more than I do. I did go to Bloomingdale's when I first arrived here, however. A woman had said to me, "You can't consider yourself an American unless you've been to Bloomingdale's." So, I took her at her word and we decided to pay the store a visit together. Unfortunately, it was the Saturday before Christmas and the shop was full to bursting. Even so, one dutiful assistant spent endless amounts of time with my friend, spraying various perfumes on her wrist and inviting her to sniff them. She was inexhaustibly polite despite being under tremendous pressure and rushed off her feet.

"A bit too sharp? A bit too acid?" She would say, "Shall we try something a bit more floral?"

The service was excellent though the experience was harrowing because every five seconds you would be barged by a forgetful husband who was rushing to find a last minute gift for his wife or girlfriend.

The shops in London are not the same. Except for Harrods. In Harrods, much like in an American shop, you can do no wrong. But mostly English people do not like to be of service, so public servants typically all behave badly. Shopkeepers and sales assistants are no different. They don't like you and they resent you if you haven't seen exactly what it is you want. They will stand in front of you thinking, but not saying, "But it's all there, for God's sake. Make up your mind." It's much easier to shop in America though I recommend avoiding such places in the week before Christmas.

Having said that I never shop, I do make one exception. Since I appeared in an advertisement for Mr. Klein[42], I do feel an obligation to be loyal to him. As such I always wear Calvin Klein briefs even though the advertisement I appeared in was for the fragrance ck one. Sadly, Mr. Klein doesn't give me the underwear for free, so I have to go into shops and buy it from time to time. They're the only thing I have ever bought in the way of clothing my whole life. I couldn't even tell you what size I buy. Small, I would think. Anyway, they are very comfortable.

Being dependent on gifts from others for my clothes does mean that I sometimes accept items I end up not actually wearing. Some coats are too heavy for me, others simply don't match anything else in my wardrobe no matter how I squint when I look in the mirror. The trouble is I can't seem to say no. It has been my mantra my whole life, even when it is to my detriment.

I never say no to anything because I am told that as I lie dying on an iron bedstead in a rented room, I shall not regret anything I did. Instead, I shall regret what I didn't do. Therefore I say yes to everything in the hope of never having any regrets. I shall be just like Madame Piaf[43].

I don't think you should ever say no to anything especially invitations or requests from others. I never decline because I feel that if I have come from England and been allowed to live in America I should be giving something back in return.

---

42 Calvin Klein, American fashion designer, b. 1942
43 Édith Piaf, French cabaret singer, songwriter and actress, 1915-1963

Of course, saying yes to everything can get you in just as much trouble as saying no. I have now learned that the opposite of saying yes is not in fact no. It is saying, "I am not worthy." which is a nicer way of saying no. You see, if someone says, "Will you marry me?" and you say, "No." it's unkind. Or if someone says, "Will you accept this great gift?" and you say, "No." then they will think, "Who does he think he is?" But if you say, "I am not worthy." then they go away content. They think, "Oh, that was nice." And it's quite a long time before they think realize it still means no.

CHAPTER 7

Living a Long Life

I'VE OFTEN WONDERED ABOUT MY longevity and what has made it possible for me to have lived so long. Principally, I think the answer is that I never asked anything of myself that is more than I can logically give. I don't stay up when I feel tired even if the company and conversation are good. I don't eat when I'm feeling full even if the food tastes good. I don't continue to drink when I find myself getting drunk. I don't walk when I find that I can't walk anymore. But it was never my aim to live for as long as I have.

I've never been a smoker. When I was young, there was still a social distinction which meant that, after a meal, the ladies would rise and go off into the drawing room, leaving the men to stay and smoke cigars or cigarettes and talk about politics and money. If you were a man and couldn't take an interest in politics or money, you were an outsider. Consequently, I was an outsider. I would sit in those smoke-filled rooms after dinner while the other men talked. I never listened. I couldn't follow the conversations. I wanted to be in the drawing room with the women.

I may have smoked once, but only to prove to myself, and whoever was watching me, that I wasn't a child. I never smoked in adult life. I didn't think it would suit me. All that stain on your fingers and on your upper lip and, of course, the smell. I didn't like it. I've asked people why they smoke and I've had some of the strangest answers. "I smoke because I'm lonely." "I used to smoke because I wanted to seem sophisticated." "I smoked because I didn't know what to do with my hands." These are problems I have never encountered, let alone sought to solve by lighting up a cigarette.

Smoking is a waste of money. People spend a fortune on cigarettes. When I lived in London, even some of my poorest friends smoked. Many of them would borrow money from me in order to buy cigarettes and, of course, they would never pay me back. I had no money as it was, but they wanted me to lend them ten shillings so that they could smoke. Of course, they and all those men who talked about politics and money are all dead now and I am still alive. Is it because I never smoked cigarettes? I suppose it might be.

Aside from avoiding excess, I know I do many things that doctors say I shouldn't. I never eat the right food, I simply eat what I am given. I never take any exercise either. Yet here I still am. I think you have to have stamina to live a long life. If you haven't got the stamina, you'd better not try because it's simply not possible to take a break somewhere along the way. It's an all-or-nothing proposition.

In some ways I was uniquely unprepared for living a long life. Had I known how long I would live for, I wouldn't have said as much as I did early on. Perhaps I could have published *The Naked Civil Servant* in two parts to eek it out a bit. If you know you're going to live a long time you should say very little and remember what it is that you do say. Otherwise you're doomed to repeat yourself over and over again as I do.

As I think I said earlier, memory is one of the first things to go. I remember a lot about the distant past, but I don't remember much about the immediate past. Chiefly, I remember what people have said rather than what they did or what they wore or looked like. My brain seems to be wired to remember words and this may account for my having such a large vocabulary. I've certainly never studied a dictionary. I think I liked words from very early on in my life though, even in my childhood I liked what were called 'grown-up words' and used them often.

There is no great secret to living in New York City as a ninety-year-old. You simply do what you would do if you lived in any city. The point of living in New York is the people. They speak to you wherever you are and you have to be ready to reply. You cannot brush people off as it takes a great effort for them to speak to you. They say to me, "I've never spoken to you before. I didn't dare."

And I ask, "What did you think would happen?"

And they don't know. I suppose they might fear me shouting at them, "Go away." or, "Don't speak to me." or something like that. But I would never say such things. I gladly speak to anyone. I even allow a certain amount of waylaying time when I go out in case I have to stop and speak to people on the way to an appointment.

Even the city's homeless people stop me although it's more often for money than my fame. I don't think they ask me for money because I'm famous. Nevertheless, I always carry with me a certain amount of giving-away money, chiefly quarters, which I give to the people who ask for it. Someone once told me it's bad to give homeless people money. They say I'm encouraging them to lead mendicant[44] lives instead of pulling themselves together and getting a job. I don't buy this argument. I know that they have been without jobs for so long that you'd have to teach them how to actually have a job long before you taught them a particular skill or trade.

In a way, the homeless are like me. I have always lived in poverty because I had no capacity to earn a living. I had no capacity to command other people and that's where the money is. When you are the company director, you earn more money than when you are a stenographer. So you are always at the losing end if you're 'a born victim' because that's the nature of society. I was commanded by everybody. I could never tell anybody what to do because I didn't know how to do it.

The key benefit of the above however is that you're never to blame, which means you seldom feel guilty about anything. This might be another clue to my longevity. I have lived a guilt-free life. If you simply do what you're told and you do the thing wrong, it's not your fault because the only thing you could have done wrong was not to have obeyed the command you were given.

---

44 Given to begging

During my brief tenure as a wage earner, I was very seldom to blame for anything unless when told to do something, I didn't do it adequately. That would have annoyed my slave drivers and afterwards I'd be given the sack. I got the sack so often that in the end I became a freelancer. You can't sack a freelancer. You can only refuse to give them more work.

My life was poorer as a freelancer, but it was much easier. My time was my own because I could decide when I wanted to do my work within the constraints of meeting whatever deadline I'd been given. When you are a freelancer, you're either rushed off your feet or else you can't think how to fill in the time. Somehow I managed to go on like that for years. When I finally gave up being a freelancer, I got a job in the art department of a publisher. After that I moved to another job in a display firm. That's when I worked in Greek Street in London's Soho.

I enjoyed working in display and the location of my employer suited my extracurricular activities perfectly. I was also their only employee. I had two bosses, both of whom were women. It was just the three of us. I did everything, more or less. They treated me almost as an equal and were very friendly. They weren't at all superior or bossy.

When I freelanced, I worried all the time about money because I only just had enough to live on. These days I manage somewhat better. Although I don't have much, it would be nice if I could take what money I have managed to accumulate with me when I die. Of course, I can't. I shall leave it to my nieces instead. It would be a pity to give all my money to the British or American government even though it was the British government that kept me until I was seventy-two and the American government that let me spend the twilight of my life here. I have managed to save a not inconsiderable amount of my earnings over the years[45]. It would have been a mistake to spend it. Money is really for hoarding or for giving away, not for spending.

Many people ask me if I have any advice on what they should do with their finances. I have no advice. My money is in the bank and I never understand it. In England banking is a cottage industry. You can go into a bank and say to the girl behind the counter, "Is he in?"

And she says, "I'll see."

If he is, the bank manager that is, he'll see you. You never get to see the bank manager of an American bank. Take my bank on Madison Avenue, for example. It's the size of a cathedral and it's manned by black ladies so elegant that their ankles are no wider than other people's wrists. I once said to one of these women, "I seem to have two accounts with your bank."

And she said, "That is correct."

When I inquired of her, "Why do I have two accounts?"

She said, "I think you need an accountant."

I left the bank none the wiser and told the whole sad story to a Mr. Engel, a sculptor who at the time was making me immortal in bronze. He said, "Have my accountant."

---

45 Quentin had over $1.25m in savings and investments at the time of his death

So, I did. I went to his accountant who was like a vast hamster living in a nest of shredded paper. I've never seen him take unpaid income tax demands and put them into his cheeks, but I'm convinced that's what he must do. The other day he said to me, "I recognize now that you're a hopeless case."

He told me I have to pay two lots of income tax, four times a year. I could never do it without his help. I wouldn't know what to send where on what day or anything. He arranges it all for me.

I've no idea what happens to my money when I put it in the bank. I assume they keep it in a pile somewhere. Occasionally I receive a note saying that I'm overdrawn. Upon receiving this I run all the way to the bank, fling myself into a chair opposite the bank manager's desk, weep and pray for death. This is apparently unnecessary.

The bank manager simply says, "Oh, don't worry. It can be readjusted." This I find extraordinary. In England, if you become overdrawn, your name is mud. You become an outcast from everything. So, I never understand it, but I float along nonetheless and I seem to be doing alright. Financial prowess is definitely not key to living a long life.

The trouble with banks is however, as I think I've explained before, that the people who work in banks are like nuns. Nuns are moved from nunnery to nunnery, or from post to post, so that they don't form a relationship with someone more important and binding than their relationship with You-Know-Who. It seems to me that banks do the same thing. Just as you think you're getting to know your bank manager, they whisk him or her off somewhere else so that he or she doesn't get too attached to you and lend you more money than they otherwise should. In my eighteen years of dealing with banks I think I have had a different bank manager every year.

Every time I get a new bank manager I have to explain myself all over again, which is not easy when you have a story like mine to tell. They're worse than dealing with doctors and I've had five of those during my time in New York.

The other day I received a letter from my bank containing a check of mine, which had the word 'void' stamped across it. I couldn't understand it. The check was for $255 or something and I had $60,000 in my checking account. Anyway, I've torn it up. If whomever the check was payable to wants the money I'm sure they'll contact me again.

I don't have any credit cards because I would hate to run into debt. I was once given a Visa card by my agent, but I never used it because I couldn't fathom how on earth I would. I know people have them. What are they for? I have noticed however, that when I go into shops and, say, spend more than twenty dollars, the shop assistant seems to get very worried nowadays when they realize I'm paying in cash. Perhaps they think they will be robbed if they keep too much cash in the till.

The only time my Visa card was any use was when I was due to catch a plane to go to Washington and I lost my ticket. The airline representative said she couldn't issue me a replacement ticket and that I would have to buy another one instead. Of course, I wasn't carrying enough cash with me to pay for a ticket. So I took the Visa card out of my pocket and asked her, "Will this do?"

And she smiled and said, "Yes."

Then she put it in a funny thing that started blinking and making some odd noises and then she gave it back to me along with a new ticket. I don't entirely know what happened, but I made my flight, which was a good thing.

I'm aware however that people seem to run up large debts through using credit cards. The television is full of advertisements at the moment for people who will take over your credit card debts and combine them all together. That way you end up owing one person a large sum of money instead of owing smaller sums to lots of companies. I don't see why that's an advantage, but as you might imagine money is a complete mystery to me.

Every year I ask the authorities in England if I owe them any tax. I do this when they send me an account of how my old age pension has accumulated in London. They never reply so it seems to be free money. I love money. Probably because I've never had much of it. If I had my way the money I have would be stored in the form of great gold coins the size of dinner plates, all lying side by side in a bank vault somewhere. I don't want my money invested. 'Invest' seems to me to be another word for 'gamble' and that is yet another thing that I wouldn't do since 'gamble' is another name for 'lose'.

Now, of course, everybody is dead. My agent is dead. My accountant is dead. Mr. Marvell[46] wrote a poem that begins,

---

46 Andrew Marvell, English poet and satirist, 1621-1678

"They are all gone into a world of light and I alone sit grieving here." Ms. Clausen[47] once said, "Writing is rewriting." She should know. I do not think of her often. I thought of her when everyone was so angry when I said a woman could abort her fetus if she knew it was gay. She would have understood what I meant.

The kinky papers for which I worked have both folded. I worked for both *The New York Native*[48] and for *Christopher Street*[49]. They were both part of an empire built up by a very resourceful man called Mr. Steele[50]. Both publications came to an end when kinkiness became mainstream. Nowadays, nobody has to read the shocking things that the *Native* or *Christopher Street* printed, they can read them in the *Wall Street Journal* or the *Sunday Times*. That put an end to Mr. Steele's kingdom, which I thought was sad. He started both of those newspapers when he was barely thirty and to be a kinky version of Mr. Murdoch[51] is no small achievement, so it is a pity that it all came to nothing.

Asked if I feel like a cat with nine lives, I say that I feel I've been very lucky. Really however, I am more akin to a dog than a cat because I have given myself over to the whims of other people time and again. I used to joke that when I signed on to be part of Mr. Lago's *Authors on Tour*, I sold myself into

---

47 Connie Clausen, Quentin's literary agent, 1923-1997
48 A biweekly gay newspaper published in New York City from 1980-1997.
49 A gay-oriented magazine published from 1976-1995.
50 Thomas Steele
51 Rupert Murdoch, Australian-born media magnate, b. 1931

slavery. I didn't mean for it to sound unkind, but he took offence at my saying it.

People have said to me, "Don't you mind being taken to places and told to sit and perform as though you were a dog?" To me it is an absurd question. It means I am never to blame for whatever I am doing or wherever I am. That's the situation I like. No one can ever sue me.

Suing is a very American occupation. Everyone sues everyone in America. One of the late Mr. Hudson's[52] ex-lovers sued his estate claiming he had not been informed when Mr. Hudson knew he had AIDS. The man in question[53] was later tested and found to be HIV negative. Nevertheless he was still awarded a sum of twenty-two million dollars. Of course, the lawyers probably ended up taking half of it and the IRS probably took the other half, but the whole thing was still extraordinary.

I have never sued anyone. I don't really understand the law. For instance, that woman[54] who cut off her husband's[55] penis was acquitted. I mean, I regard that as one of the most terrible crimes I have ever heard of. Yet people stood outside the court and cheered when she was acquitted. She was said to be insane. This seems odd to me. Mr. Dahmer[56] was said to be sane, but he cut up small boys while they were still alive and

---

52 Rock Hudson, American leading man and actor, 1925-1985
53 Marc Christian (born Marc Christian MacGinnis)
54 Lorena Bobbitt, b. 1970
55 John Wayne Bobbitt, b. 1967
56 Jeffrey Dahmer, American serial killer and sex offender, 1960-1994

stuffed them in the refrigerator. I think even he made soup out of them. Does that seem to be the action of a sane person? I don't think so.

When I am asked about my life's legacy, I have to admit I don't think I'm really leaving anything behind for anyone. I have tried to do right by the people I've met, but of course you seldom really know what is good for people. If you are not careful you give people what you think they deserve and that's a bad idea. I think my legacy is principally nothing. As Keats[57] said, when I have gone "My name will be written in water". Very few people do such good deeds that they really leave people with something tangible. Someone like Edison[58] really did do something for the world. He changed it for the better. I mean we have cities which are lit by electricity from end to end and that would have been inconceivable without him. When he died, they say he held more than a thousand patents. The nice thing about his achievements, I suppose, was that he could see the difference he made in his own lifetime.

I've certainly noticed the world changing during my lifetime, though it's not because of anything that I have done or said. People have grown more open. They feel they can say more about themselves than previous generations could. I don't know if that's a good thing, but they probably benefit by having said it rather than keeping everything a secret.

---

57 John Keats, English romantic poet, 1795-1821

58 Thomas Edison, American inventor of the phonograph, the motion picture camera, and the practical electric light bulb, 1847-1931

When I was young, people had so many secrets. Secrets about their family. Secrets about themselves. Secrets about their marriage. Now there are almost no secrets. Everybody knows everything about everyone and they don't seem to judge you as much. In the past people feared they would never be able to show their face in public again. Yes, I can definitely say that over the course of my lifetime, though the world may have gotten worse, the people have gotten better.

Yes, people are still impatient, but to my mind they are more civic-minded rather than less these days, contrary to what the newspapers say. I think they actually care more about a neighborhood than they used to. Nowadays we are forced to take other people into consideration because there are so many of us and we all live such revealed lives that you cannot help but take notice of other people.

At the same time however, we seem to be entering a new era. An era of neuroses, self-diagnosed or otherwise. This means that everyone nowadays has their own shrink. At least, everyone in America does.

To me though, psychoanalysis is just another form of self-indulgence. You see, it used to be the case that your troubles made you at one with other people. Now, it seems to be that your troubles separate you from other people. So although the world has gotten more crowded it has actually become a lonelier place.

I have never seen a psychiatrist and regard psychoanalysis as absolute rubbish. Why can't you work out your own problems? It's much better than involving someone who has never met you. I mean, you go into their room and they say, "Ah. And then? Mmm. And how did you feel about that?" You pay them for the privilege of hearing your own words repeated back at you. You might as well go and share your problems with a cave.

Personally, I don't believe in help from other people unless it's technical. When you're ill, I think you can go to a doctor and he can say, "Your liver doesn't work." You wouldn't have thought of that and the medicine he or she prescribes for you works and does you good. But ordinary human problems can be answered by anybody, foremost amongst them, yourself.

I suppose my legacy, if I have one, is the same as that of all others who have lived longer than the average person around him or her. It is the commentary I can provide that bears witness to the great changes that sweep through society. I can remind others of where society came from and the direction in which we are heading. Observing others has been the preoccupation of my long and otherwise unproductive life. I was twenty-two years old when Edison died.

CHAPTER 8

The Twenty-First Century

IF I HAD A VISION of the twenty-first century, and I assure you
that I do not, I would have to say that I think things will generally get worse. That seems to me to be the trend that time
is taking.

Everything in my lifetime has got louder, cheaper, faster,
nastier and sexier, and I don't think it will suddenly reverse
itself and go in the opposite direction. Of course, the world
becoming louder, cheaper, faster, nastier and sexier is not
a good thing, but I shan't be around. So long as the world
doesn't become sufficiently loud that it wakes me from the
long sleep that lies ahead of me, I shan't care.

Generally, I would think that the twenty-first century will
be much like the century that is now passing. As I write this,
everyone is worried about planes falling from the sky when
the clocks tick over to January 1, 2000. It would certainly
be a novel way of ringing in the new year. We shall all be at
New Year's parties when the Times Square ball falls, whereupon perhaps we shall all be plunged into darkness with all
the machines around us exploding and showering us with

91

debris. If I am at a party, I think I will make a point of heading home and going to bed early. If I am to be crushed by a falling Boeing 747, I would rather be tucked up in bed when it happens.

In addition to worrying about the 'millennium bug'[59], everyone appears to be coming down with what has been described as 'millennium fever'. My understanding of 'millennium fever' is that people are even more anxious than usual to celebrate the dawning of a new year since it also represents a new millennium. This, of course, is nonsense. The year 2000 does not represent the passing of another thousand years. The third millennium won't actually start until January 1, 2001. Moreover, the point from which we are counting seems to me to be entirely arbitrary. In effect we're celebrating two thousand years since the entirely undocumented date of birth of some half-starved fanatic from the Middle East. I don't know why it's so significant.

It's been explained to me that 'the millennium' is just an excuse for having a huge party. This I accept, although it can only lead to disappointment. More likely than not, I shall not attend any kind of party this New Year's Eve. I know people like them though. They go out into the street and set off fireworks and then everybody embraces everybody. I'm lucky enough that I can embrace everybody without the need for a party. Nevertheless, assuming we are not all bitten by the 'millennium bug', revelers will doubtless wake up on January 1,

---

59 A concern that computer systems reliant on a two-digit readout for years would not be able to handle the transition from 99, representing 1999, to 00, being the year 2000.

2000, with the same hangover they had last year and the same feeling of anticlimax and disappointment. New Year's celebrations are always the same. This year however, I suppose it will just make a bigger dent in people's bank balances.

With luck, I will die before the millennium. I haven't made any plans to celebrate my ninety-first birthday in December. Presumably if I do make it to my birthday, any celebrations will be smaller than the ones for my ninetieth. I hope I do not live to be one hundred. Ten more years of this would be unbearable.

As someone that has seen, first hand, most of the twentieth century, I would have to say that the atom bomb was the greatest invention of the hundred years from 1900 to 2000. Now, we all live in Terrorland because fissionable material exists and will, at some stage, fall into the wrong hands. In fact, I know a man whose job is to fly about the world buying up fissionable material so that it doesn't fall into the clutches of wicked people. 'Wicked people' are always the people who would use such technology and devices against us. We are never 'wicked people'. Ours are never the wrong hands.

I don't have a clear memory of the date when the first atom bomb was dropped on Hiroshima[60], but I do remember reading Mr. Hersey's[61] article in *The New Yorker*, which took up the magazine. The second bomb somehow never took off the same

---

60 August 6, 1945

61 John Hersey, Pulitzer Prize-winning American journalist whose account of the aftermath of the atomic bomb dropped on Hiroshima, Japan, is arguably one of the finest pieces of American journalism, 1914-1993

way the first one did. I don't know why. Maybe because the second one was a sin because the Japanese had sued for peace before the second bomb was dropped. These days no one ever remembers Nagasaki or ever refers to it. History rarely offers prizes for those who come second.

When I say that the atom bomb was the greatest invention of the twentieth century, I obviously don't mean to say that those who died in Japan deserved death or that their deaths are any cause for celebration. I merely mean to say that no other invention in recent times has had such an effect on our way of living. The cold war was all about mutually assured destruction and none of that would have taken place if it wasn't for the atom bomb. World War II would not have ended in the manner it did. So really, the invention of the atom bomb shaped the entire second half of the twentieth century and continues to influence us to this day.

The computer is, of course, another great invention of the twentieth century, though at the moment I wouldn't say that its effect has been as far-reaching as the atom bomb. Maybe in time, that will change.

Hand in hand with the computer, of course, came the Internet. In theory, the fact that we can now all know one another and communicate with one another is a wonderful thing. In practice however, it all seems to be getting very nasty. The Internet seems to be being used to facilitate people's sexual desires, desires that previously were muted by the effort needed to find like-minded people to share in such exploits. The Internet seems to have made it easier for perverts to find each other and for pornography of every shape, color and persuasion to be just a click away. Perhaps, once everyone has gotten their kicks, people will find more constructive ways to use the Internet.

When the computer was invented, they must have thought how wonderful it would be that everyone could be in touch with everybody else. Were someone to shout, "Help." thousands of people would hear. If someone were to shout, "I'm lonely." millions of like-minded people would be able to reply and new friendships would be made. But, of course, what has happened is that people are using it for purely sexual purposes and now everyone worries because they think our children will end up being corrupted as a result.

The inventors of the Internet seemed to think that their invention would help build a sort of global community, but being connected to the Internet is not the same as living in a town. Towns are typically fairly small, which gives you a sense of identity. The Internet is so large and contains so many people that I think it's hard for people to feel anything other than lost and insignificant when interacting with it. For the Internet to help people I think it needs to somehow be made smaller and more relevant to people's lives.

I read a story in the papers the other day about Mr. Pound[62] who supported the Nazis and Mussolini during World War II despite being born an American. He was arrested in Italy when it was liberated and was later charged by the American forces

---

62 Ezra Pound, American poet and critic, 1885-1972

for treason. It reminded me of how much we didn't know about the war until afterwards. It's unthinkable nowadays in the age of cable news and the Internet, but we didn't know anything about The Holocaust until much later.

As I reach the end of my life, I have to conclude that most of the harm done in the world is done by those who think they know what happiness is for other people and try to help them achieve it. If everyone was preoccupied with themselves there would be much less harm done.

Happiness is, of course, getting what you want, but the secret of happiness is learning that it's easier to like what you have. If you wake every morning and say to yourself, "I am nothing. I deserve nothing." then everything that happens after that is a bonus. It's people who think they deserve something that end up unfulfilled, let down, angry and unhappy. Part of being happy is about ceasing restlessness or the notion that there is always something better around the corner or something that you're missing out on.

Once more I have digressed a little so let me end this chapter with what I started, namely why I think the twenty-first century will be louder, cheaper, faster, nastier and sexier than the hundred years that preceded it. Let me start with louder.

Since Edison invented the phonograph, later called the gramophone, life has gotten noisier. Television followed as did the jet engine. And now, of course, we have more human beings on the planet using all the devices and contraptions that man has made. If mankind's output were measured in decibels, our species must surely be producing record amounts of noise. This can only mean one thing: we must all be getting collectively deafer. This, in turn, will surely mean we will all have to shout and be shouted at just to hear one another in the future and our music will have to be played even louder just for us to hear it.

The good news is that ear plugs, along with everything else you might care to buy, are becoming cheaper and cheaper. At the beginning of the twentieth century the idea that every household would have a car, several televisions and foreign holidays was laughable. Yet, nowadays, a child grows up expecting not only each of these but much, much more. Everything in the future will be cheaper still, though doubtless the average American will still not have enough and will still yearn for more.

Although most major cities are stuck in gridlock these days, people in the twentieth century will also find their lives moving faster and faster. Cellular phones are already injecting lives with an immediacy hitherto unheard of. This will only get worse as people struggle to do more and more. Doubtless this will lead to more nervous breakdowns, more hip replacements and more accidents. It should be hoped that people will be more content through doing more, but history has shown that this is seldom the case.

It truth, it is hard to know if the world has gotten nastier in the twentieth century, or if the television news stations have just gotten better at reporting the gruesome details of the latest war, kidnapping or murder. It would be nice to think that the world will not allow events like The Holocaust to be repeated, but of course recent events in Rwanda have shown just how slow we are to learn from past mistakes. Generally however, I expect the twenty-first century to be nastier than the twentieth. The Internet is chiefly to blame for this, although computer games are surely just as culpable. It would be nice to think that there is no evil in the world and that all disagreements are really just exercises in misunderstanding. This is not the case. There are people in the world who genuinely wish others harm and the Internet will bring them together and offer them anonymity. Moreover, if history proves nothing else, it shows that over time, humans become more and more inventive when it comes to ways to harm each other.

Lastly, the twenty-first century will be sexier than any period before it. As we entered the twentieth century, women were afraid to show their ankles. These days, women's vaginas practically have their own webpages. In order to be a movie star in the twenty-first century, you will need to look like a porn star as films become more and more risqué. These days, sex sells everything from underwear to chewing gum and soap powder and it is a winning formula that will continue to marginalize the prudish, the plain-looking and the elderly.

Whereas in the twentieth-century there was a distinction between men and women, in the twenty-first century the lines of gender will become more and more blurred. I am thankful I shall not be around to see it. Not because I think people that live in the twenty-first century won't enjoy their lives, I have no doubt that they will, but because there comes a point in your life when you realize you are just not cut out for modern living. Your values are old-fashioned. *You* are old-fashioned, and that's okay.

All that I ask is that you keep the noise down to an acceptable level.

CHAPTER 9

The Trappings of Notoriety

FAME, I FIND, IS A particularly American pastime. I hesitate to describe myself as famous, but since fame is something that people, particularly Americans, are interested in, it has been suggested to me that I should write about it here.

I struggle with the question "Why am I famous?" Although I have expressed opinions about the world at large in my writing, I hesitate to call myself a philosopher. All I really do is talk about myself. I am aware however, that I have a story-telling voice and this I think comes across in my writing and when I am talking to people. When I tell a story, I tell it like stories should be told. I don't have it forced out of me in bits and pieces. I begin at the beginning and I go all the way through to the end.

I think I enjoy hearing my own voice, even though I think I have an ugly voice. More probably, I just enjoy the fact that people are willing to listen to me. I remember Mrs. Churchill[63] saying of parties that we were both at, "In the beginning people

---

63 June Churchill, a friend of Quentin's

speak to one another and then, after a while, only Quentin is speaking and everyone is listening to him." I bowed my head in shame when I heard this because, of course, I shouldn't do that.

Story telling isn't something that men typically do, in my opinion. When you ask a man, "What happened?" men do not gather around to listen to the story. Women do. They huddle together and then one will begin, "Well, I was walking down the street…" And you can tell they are beginning a story.

Men will say, "Well, I don't know."

And you will prompt him by asking, "Tell us what happened."

And he will say, "Well, nothing much."

And he will have to have the saga dragged out of him at great reluctance.

Certainly my ability to tell a tale is, perhaps, the one skill I have that has contributed to my rise to notoriety. I prefer to think of myself as notorious because people that are famous are famous for a reason. People that are notorious are famous for no reason. Or no good reason.

Another explanation for my notoriety is my willingness to have my picture taken. I enjoy being photographed a great deal and when I am being photographed I will posture this way and that. I prefer being asked if I will give permission to have my photo taken because typically people look awful when they are photographed unaware or unprepared. You end up looking like a human being, which is not the point at all. I must confess however, that these days I am tired of being photographed because now they tend to take so many. If they only take a few pictures, that's fine. If I'm only with them for half an hour, that's wonderful. But if I am with them for too long, I get tired of it.

Being recognized on the street can be tricky. Many a time I've been walking home when I've realized someone is trying to take my picture. They end up walking backwards in front of you. I don't like being photographed while I walk because I feel like I have to walk a certain way. I can't stumble, but I can't look at the pavement to see where I'm walking because I have to keep my head up. You have to walk in a very blithe, breezy, airy way, which at my age takes some doing.

When I do live performances, I have no problem with photographers using flashes. I understand this makes me almost unique among live performers, though this may be because I know my one-man show back to front and left to right. It strikes me that photographers using flash bulbs are more prone to upset members of my audience rather than me.

When I was performing at the Duke of York's Theatre in London, one photographer kept taking photos all through the performance and every time she took a photo her camera's flash went off. Anyway, when we got to the question and answer part of the show one of the audience members asked me, "Can't you stop the person using flashlight photography?"

To which I answered, "I will try." And I looked up at the box where the photographer in question was sitting and said, "And that means you." and she stopped.

I know that in some theatres they have notices that read "No part of this performance may be photographed or recorded." Whether that's to prevent the show from being shown to people who have not paid for a seat, or whether it's to keep the performers or audience at ease, I don't know.

I never was photographed by Mr. Mapplethorpe.[64] I don't think I had the right equipment for such an undertaking, but I've been photographed by various people over the years, some of them very important.

I remember being photographed by Mr. Scavullo[65] and him being very efficient. He takes you into a room which is white: the floor is white, the ceiling is white and the walls are white. And they are all joined by a process which has no edge, so that the floor curves and becomes one with the walls and the ceiling.

In the middle of the room there's a little red cross on the floor and he says, "Stand there." And you put one foot on that and he is fed with cameras by his assistant. He stretches out his hand, a camera is placed into it and he photographs you. You quickly realize that if he stands still, you move. And if he moves, you stand still. You only have to move a little bit. People always say, "I never know what to do when I'm photographed," but you don't have to do anything. You just sit or stand there and go into a pose.

On another occasion I was photographed by Greg Gorman[66] and when I saw the photographs I thought how wonderful

---

64 Robert Mapplethorpe, American photographer, 1946-1989

65 Francesco Scavullo, American fashion photographer, 1921-2004

66 Greg Gorman, American portrait photographer of Hollywood celebrities, b. 1949

they were. But mostly you just accept your photographs as they are. I don't really care what I look like. If photographers say, "We'll show you the photographs," I'll say, "Oh, that's nice," but if they forget, it doesn't bother me.

Friction only seems to occur when a photographer and his subject disagree on how the subject should look. Photographers typically want to be in control of their image and subjects typically want to be in control of how they are seen.

Of course if I were a movie star, I would have to care what I look like. I mean, we say we're all above all that, but actors and actresses can't afford to be above it. You cannot release photographs in which you look absolutely terrible, and you have an assistant, an agent, and studio heads and everything, so you are watched over like a hawk. And I suppose, in the end movie stars end up believing that they look in real life the way they do on the screen. I would imagine that's hard for them to deal with.

I realize now that I look old. When I first arrived in America, I did not look as old and I was able to disguise the fact that I looked old. Ms. Loy[67] used to hold her head higher and higher to prevent the shadows under her chin from showing in photographs. I sort of regret looking old, in a vague way, but I don't sit in my room chewing my nails, worrying about it. I've had to let vanity go. I haven't thrown it anywhere. It's been taken from my hands.

The other day a gentleman rang me up and said he was an officer of Madame Tussauds, the waxworks company, and

---

67 Myrna Loy, American film, television and stage actress, 1905-1993

that they were going to open a venue on Times Square and would I permit them to make a waxwork figure of me. The venue, of course, instantly made the proposition raffish, since Times Square is associated with peep shows, strip joints, and such other delightful places. Apparently, however, it is now being cleaned up and made respectable.

Madame Tussauds has, of course, a museum in London, which I visited once when I lived there. I remember going down into the Chamber of Horrors where Mary Queen of Scots was constantly being beheaded. Upstairs however, there were waxworks of all the crowned heads of state standing about in their royal robes and in the next room there were stage and film stars.

Quite why they want to make a waxwork imitation of me, I can't imagine, but, as is my policy, I naturally said yes. Whom they shall stand me in between, I can't imagine. Perhaps the Mayflower Madame[68] will be on one side and Mrs. Simpson[69] will be on the other.

They took me to a place that was sort of like a hotel in which they had hired a room for the day. Then they sat me in a chair and questioned me about everything I wore and the type of makeup I have on my face. They then asked me to give them my clothes, which I declined to do because I have so few. In the end I gave them my black velvet jacket which I don't

68 Sydney Biddle Barrows, American known as the 'Mayflower Madam' because she ran an escort agency, b. 1952

69 Wallis Simpson, American socialite whose third husband, King Edward VIII, abdicated his throne to marry her, 1896-1986

wear as often as I used to. I couldn't give them my hat because I don't have another.

I was less frightened of the physical treatment that awaited me. This is because of my background being a model for sculpture classes in art schools. They pressed instruments against my cheekbones to measure the width of face, then they measured my forehead to see at what point my hairline started followed by the distance between the top of my head and my chin to ascertain how long my face is. It took at least two or three hours to get everything done. They were very nice to me and gave me cups of coffee the whole time. It will apparently take at least two years before Times Square's Madame Tussauds opens[70]. I doubt I will be around to see it, but at least when it does I shall be immortalized as a waxwork.

Did I set out to be famous? Of course not. I was at the mercy of the world for far too long. Personally, I think that life itself just happens, and we make of it what we can. Those people who are a success in life are the people who sorted out very early what they wanted to do and had the capacity to do it. That wasn't me. I have just been lucky to live long enough to see the meagre seeds that I planted grow and bear fruit.

There are lots of people who want to be great dancers. They do not have the ability to be great dancers, but they won't give up going to dancing lessons and attending auditions. I once knew a girl in London who went to an endless number of auditions and was always very angry because she had never

---

70 The grand opening was on November 15, 2000

been chosen. I said to her, "You must find some way of earning a living off of the stage."

To which she replied, "Why should I?"

I couldn't sway her, but I knew perfectly well she was going to reach middle age and be a failed actress instead of being a successful 'something else'. I don't know what became of her. When I ceased going to the café she frequented, I ceased to see her.

I do think I have had a great deal of luck. For instance, most recently when my hand became paralyzed and I couldn't type anymore, I had to give up the profession of writing. That happened at the exact moment that I met Mr. Lago who said, "Will you be part of *Authors on Tour*?" and I went into the speaking profession almost immediately. I have had these strange coincidences in my life which I can't explain other than to say that they are luck.

Although I have previously stated that I am a victim of fate, I do admit to having pushed fate around a little bit so that I never starved or went bankrupt. After I'd written *The Naked Civil Servant,* an art master said to me, "What are you going to do now?" to which I replied, "I shall lean forward so that fate can see me."

I think I have a good idea of how the *world* sees me, good and bad, because I receive endless hate letters alongside my fan mail. At first, I was surprised to learn that there were people I'd never met that hated me, but then after a while I thought, "Well, why am I surprised?" The strange thing is, if you're told someone likes you, you bow your head and lower your eyelids and smile. When you are told they don't like you, you say "Why?" For some reason we all expect everyone to like us without question, yet we, more than anyone else, know our own faults and foibles.

One of the hate letters I received said I was preoccupied with my fleeting fame. In a way, I am preoccupied with it because I am mystified by it. I don't take it for granted though because I can't see why it's there. I think it's important that you do not take your fame for granted. You should always seem grateful for anything that happens to you because you're famous.

I think one arrives at the profession of being. You have to earn it and work away at it. You have to give up what you usually do for work and you have to float yourself confidently, feeling that you will succeed and that people will support you and help you and lift you up. It's like setting out on sea voyage without a boat. I shouldn't think you can achieve it when you're young, but you might be able to if you were, for instance, a child star.

It was not until I came to America that I truly arrived at the profession of being. I was seventy-two when I arrived and it's only because I have lived so long that I've been able to enjoy it. Most people are dead by the time they're seventy-five.

One of the trappings of notoriety that I enjoy the most is my correspondence with others. Principally this takes place in the form of letters, but since my number is listed in the telephone directory I also receive a large number of phone calls as well.

Most of the letters I receive are from women, which tends to surprise a lot of people. There is a good reason for this: women are the chief letter writers. Men never write them so you never receive any from them. I like anyone that takes the time to write to me and I feel it is my duty to respond to each and every letter that I receive. Well, not so much the hate letters. The people who send those don't tend to supply a return address.

I remember the scorn that was heaped upon me by the press when I announced, "Nobody is boring who will talk about himself." So now I instead say, "Nobody is boring who will tell the *truth* about himself." That, I think, is the key. Present yourself to the world as an accepting force, rather than a critical or scornful person and be somebody they can confide in.

I once knew a woman in England who had a husband and two children. She told me, "I write to my best friend every week."

And I asked her, "What do you say?"

And she said, "Oh, little things."

I imagined, though I didn't ask any more, that she wrote about some new fabric she'd seen in Arding & Hobbs[71] for a pound less per yard than in the shops nearby and so on. That probably made her week. And I'm sure her friend wrote back and congratulated her. Personally, I dislike resorting to trivial remarks to keep a friendship going, which brings me to one

---

71 Formerly a department store in Battersea, London, at the junction of Lavender Hill and St John's Road

of my biggest faults: although I reply to the letters I receive, I don't usually keep up a correspondence with someone once it's begun.

People write to me and I reply. Then they will write again and I won't reply because I know that if I do I am going to have to write to them once a month if I'm not careful. If I wrote three times a year to everybody who writes to me it would take up my entire life. Typically, if people write to me a second time and I don't reply, I receive a third letter which says, "Was it something I said?" That's when things become difficult. If I judge them to be young, I write back a careful letter saying, "Don't regard this letter as a reproach. I am sure people are glad to have a letter from you." Then I explain why I can't keep up a correspondence and that usually satisfies them.

My sister used to have a harrowing time at Christmas, though it was entirely of her own doing. She would receive hundreds of Christmas cards and rather than open them as they arrived, she would pin them all to a screen until, I presume, Twelfth Night, whereupon she would open them. Then she would let out screams of anguish. "Oh. I didn't send them a card." And then she would rush out to buy them a New Year's card by way of recompense. Sometimes you would hear her reprimanding herself, "But I thought they were dead."

She saw it as her duty to send Christmas cards to all of her family, friends and doubtless countless members of her husband's parish. I do not see it as my duty to write to people. It is a pleasure to write to them for the first time and I try to reply gladly in the same way that I will gladly speak to strangers, but thereafter it gets a little wearing. As I write this I still haven't answered all the letters I received at Christmas. I simply haven't had time to go through them all.

Sometimes I think people only recognize me because of my hats. If I ever left my room not wearing a hat, I'm sure very few people would recognize me. I have always liked hats. When my hair was thick and immovable, I never wore them. It was only after I was about thirty that I started putting them on my head every time I ventured out. I think that's when they became part of my persona. I like them on other people too, particularly women and Boy George.[72]

My first hat, I think, was more or less a fedora. You know those hats with curly brims which dip in front. Like the ones that gangsters used to wear. It was a light stone color and it was quite unspectacular. I don't know why I chose to wear a fedora. I suppose because it's a very masculine kind of hat. I never wore hats while my father was alive and my mother only objected to my hats because she thought I would be in danger if I made myself too conspicuous. Plus, she thought the hats would prevent me getting the oft-mentioned job she thought I needed.

My present hat, what I call my sheriff's hat, was given to me in Rochester by the owner of a hat shop who rushed out and gave it to me. "Wear this." he said, and when I put it on, it fitted me perfectly. I would say it is my favorite piece of clothing. It exactly fits my head and no amount of wind can tear

---

72 Boy George, George Alan O'Dowd, English singer, songwriter, b. 1961

it off. It's also impervious to the rain, so it acts like a kind of shield and keeps me from the elements.

Hats aside, I've never really minded what I wear. I do have a distinct style, but that's probably more about what I wouldn't wear than what I would. I have never sought to be too eye-catching. I was at a birthday party once, a long time ago, in England, and someone had given our host a tie as a present. The pattern on the tie consisted of yellow stripes, blue spots and green circles on it. Our host was aghast and asked if there was anyone in the room that would wear such a tie. To my surprise, everyone said, "We know who would. Quentin." This troubled me greatly and caused me to think very seriously about what I wore in public after that.

I have some basic rules which I think almost border on common sense. I never wear anything with a pattern on it unless the pattern's very faint. I nearly always wear plain things. I don't wear striped suits or checked suits or spotted socks or striped ties. I nearly always wear plain fabric because it seems to me you create more of an effect if you wear one color. It's like a picture; a picture is no good unless you can describe it as a blue picture or a red picture. Mr. Picasso,[73] for example, had a blue period. If you have to describe a picture as 'of various colors', to me, it somehow lessens it. I try to wear clothes that are not more spectacular than I am, so I wear black and gray and blue and so on, just to be on the safe side.

---

73 Pablo Picasso, Spanish painter and sculptor, 1881-1973

Over the years my scarves have become a bit of a trade mark for me as well. They're always given to me and seem to be a perfect gift because they can easily be put into an envelope and sent through the post. As I said before, it tends to be women that write to me rather than men and I think women tend to like scarves themselves, which is why they send them to me.

CHAPTER 10

Plays, Musicals and Operas

PERHAPS NOT SURPRISING FOR SOMEONE who has reviewed films and books during my so-called career, I have always been a great fan of the arts. What else would you expect from someone whose chief purpose in life has been to observe others? Nothing pleases me more than seeing a good play or musical although I'll confess upfront I'm not a huge fan of opera. Of course, I have seen more than my fair share of shabby productions as well as great ones, but even when I do, I smile politely and try to say nice things afterwards. It's important to remember that a poor production is never the fault of any individual person.

With very little of my life ahead of me I can say that my favorite play, the play that moved me the most, was *The Plow And The Stars* by Mr. O'Casey.[74] It was really the acting in the production I saw that made it so significant for me. The Irish Players came to London, and we English had never seen acting so naturalistic before. It was wonderful.

---

74 Sean O'Casey, Irish dramatist, 1880-1964

I was also lucky enough to see the London premier of Mr. Shaw's[75] *Saint Joan,* with Sybil Thorndike[76] playing the role of Joan of Arc, the actress for whom Shaw had written the part. She was one of the great actresses of the English stage. It was a very theatrical play. I must have been about fifteen or sixteen when I saw the production, which is probably why it left such an impression on me.

Edith Evans,[77] later Dame Edith Evans, was another brilliant English stage actress. I first saw her when I was about twenty in the restoration play *The Beaux Stratagem*[78]. At the time, I didn't know that asides, of which restoration plays are full, were spoken to the audience. I thought they were things that the actor thought in his head and spoke aloud so that the audience could hear as though he or she were thinking them. Ms. Evans made a point of leaving the cast, coming down to the footlights and saying the asides, then going back and continuing the play. It was so outrageous that it was brilliant. She was a magnificent comedian. She was completely artificial. She couldn't really play a real human being until much later by which time she had entered the movie business and had to tone it down for the silver screen.

Of course, the crowning moment of Ms. Evans' film career was when she played Lady Bracknell in a movie adaptation of Mr. Wilde's[79] play *The Importance of Being Earnest.* There is

---

75 George Bernard Shaw, Irish playwright, 1856-1950

76 Sybil Thorndike, English actress, 1882-1976

77 Dame Edith Evans, English actress, 1888-1976

78 A play by George Farquhar, Irish dramatist, 1677-1707

79 Oscar Wilde, Irish playwright, novelist and essayist, 1854-1900

a wonderful recording of her giving Wilde's famous speech, the one that begins, "Your name is not on my list and I have the same list the dear Duchess of Bolton has. Indeed, we work together."

She then questions Mr. Worthing as to whether he can be put on her list of acceptable suitors for her daughter. Then, of course, he says, "It would not be true to say that I lost my parents. They lost me. I was found."

The next few lines are paramount and you have to begin them in a very low tone, which I know from having played the role myself[80].

Lady Bracknell simply repeats everything everyone says. She says, "Found?"

Mr. Worthing elaborates, "In a cloakroom."

She echoes, "A cloakroom?"

Then he finishes with, "In a handbag."

To which Edith Evans wails, "A handbag?"

It's very funny.

Ms. Evans was a large lady and not blessed with good looks. I suppose that's why she had to act. You see, if you are very beautiful, you don't act. *Punch* magazine famously reviewed a late nineteenth century production of *The School For Scandal*[81] in which it listed members of the cast and passed judgment on their performance. At the very end of the review it stated, "Lady Teazle's clothes worn by Ms. Langtry" because Lillie

---

80 Quentin performed in the play with the Mercer Street Theatre (NYC), directed by Evan Thompson, in August and September 1982.

81 A play by Richard Sheridan, Irish satirist, playwright and poet, 1751-1816

Langtry[82] did nothing. She was so beautiful, she had only to appear. Coincidentally, it was Oscar Wilde, a close friend of Ms. Langtry's, who encouraged her to embark upon a stage career when she ran out of money.

The first play I ever saw was called *Chu Chin Chow.*[83] It was a comedy-musical and I loved it. It involved a huge cast of women dressed in Arabic dress. It was practically a pantomime, of course, but it was more of an extravaganza. You see, it's not good showing children pantomimes because children don't want political jokes. They don't get them. When a comedian comes on during a pantomime and makes a joke about the Prime Minister, children have no idea who he's talking about. Pantomimes are really for adults wanting to relive their childhood. What children want is spectacle. *Chu Chin Chow* had real camels that walked across the stage. It was mesmerizing.

As I've said, I don't particularly care for opera, but over the years I have discovered what's wrong with opera. I should also state that I've only seen a total of two operas in my lifetime. That number seems to me to be quite enough. I've seen *Porgy and Bess*[84] which I liked, and another opera that I saw by mistake. Let me explain the mistake.

I used to frequent a small New York café called Binibon which was once so terrible that there was always a table. No

---

82 Lilly Langtry, an initially beautiful young woman who established a reputation as an actress and producer, 1853-1929

83 Music by Frederic Norton, 1869-1946, book by Oscar Asche, 1871-1936

84 Music by George Gershwin, 1898-1937, libretto by DuBose Heyward, 1885-1940, and lyrics by Ira Gershwin, 1896-1983

one ever went there. Then one day I arrived to find that the place was full. Packed. There was nowhere to sit. It turned out that Mr. Mailer's little friend had stabbed one of the waiters to death[85] and, oddly, this had led to a surge in patronage. Anyway, since I couldn't get my own table, I was compelled to sit with some other people, all of whom were talking about Mr. Pavarotti[86].

I began to gibber and twitch as I do because new people to me are lovable by the pound, when all of a sudden someone said, "Would you like to go and see him?" They meant go and see Pavarotti. And hesitantly I found myself muttering, "Ye... ye... yes." I knew I *didn't* want to see him. He was a singer which is a bad thing. I was trying to be polite which is always a mistake.

So I ended up seeing *Rigoletto*[87] in which Mr. Pavarotti was playing the part of the Duke of Mantua. The opera house in which the performance was staged, The Metropolitan Opera House, was so large and our seats so bad that Mr. Pavarotti, who is very generously proportioned, was the size of a cheap postage stamp in the distance.

The plot of the opera seemed to revolve around getting Mr. Pavarotti into a sack and stabbing him. This finally happened offstage I'm happy to say. Afterwards members of the cast carried a limp bundle onstage, which we, the audience,

---

85 Norman Mailer, American novelist, playwright, film-maker and political activist, 1923-2007, in 1980 spearheaded convicted killer Jack Abbott's bid for parole. Abbott was released in June 1981 only to stab 22-year-old waiter Richard Adan to death on July 18

86 Luciano Pavarotti, Italian operatic tenor, 1935-2007

87 A three-act opera by Giuseppe Verdi, 1813-1901

were supposed to think was him. But even I, who know nothing about opera, knew that it would take at least four men and a wheelbarrow to carry on Mr. Pavarotti, dead or alive. So I cried out, "It isn't him." They paid no heed. They opened the sack and inside was the daughter of the man who had hatched the whole wicked plot. She sang and died and, to my surprise, everyone took it very seriously.

Anyway, the trouble with opera is that, first of all, the plots are too complicated. There is, for example, an opera[88] in which, before it begins, a gypsy who is to be burned alive for witchcraft commands her daughter to avenge her, so the daughter steals a baby whom everyone thinks has burned as well because baby's bones are found in the ashes of the pyre. This is before it begins.

Why don't they have simple plots? Why don't they make the temptation of Eve into an opera, then when the curtain goes up you would say, "He must be Adam, she must be Eve, and that thing in the middle must be the serpent." At least you would be able to follow it. As it is, you cannot hear the words in opera because, even if you could speak the language, the singing distorts them beyond all recognition.

Next, why do operas take place in such huge arenas? It's obvious that operas should take place in a room about the same size as a family's living room so that opera singers can sing happily, sadly and angrily as necessary. On the current stages, large as football pitches, they can only belt out the

---

88 *Il trovatore* by Giuseppe Verdi

notes as loudly as possible. No one in the audience is wondering, "I wonder if she'll marry the fat man with the beard or the fat man without a beard, or whether she will escape from prison before the end." No, they are preoccupied with whether or not a particular singer will be able to negotiate the approaching merciless top C. They wait for it and they think, "Here it comes. She got it. Hooray." It's like a circus. "Will the man catch the wrists of the other man as he flies through air? He got it. Hooray." It really is nonsense. Why are all parts written so they are just out of reach of singers? It defies logic.

Returning to more sensible theatre, I have to tell you that, in my opinion, today's theatre has lost its poetry. Now that Mr. Williams[89] is dead, I don't think theatre has anybody, really. Mr. Orton's[90] play[91] which I saw, is funny but not enlightening. It doesn't say anything that you remember. It doesn't comment on life. It only comments on a situation, which is as far-fetched as it can be. These days, I don't think theatre touches you.

I think it's sad that Broadway has taken to producing children's plays. *Cats*[92] is now the longest running show on Broadway and every member of the cast is dressed in a cat suit. It's ludicrous. Before that, I saw *Starlight Express*[93] which was about the broken hearts of railway coaches. I don't know

---

89 Tennessee Williams, American playwright, 1911-1983
90 Joe Orton, British playwright, 1933-1967
91 *Loot*, a play by Joe Orton
92 Music by Andrew Lloyd Webber, b. 1948, with lyrics by T. S. Eliot, 1888-1965, Trevor Nunn, b. 1940, and Richard Stilgoe, b. 1943
93 Music by Andrew Lloyd Webber with lyrics by Richard Stilgoe

why there are so few serious plays being put on nowadays. I'm afraid theatres are dumbing down their productions in order to appeal to the masses. They don't understand that television already does that.

I understand that Mr. Spacey[94] appeared in *The Iceman Cometh*[95] which is certainly a serious play. It lasts for about four and a half hours. I would have liked to have seen that. Of Mr. O'Neil's plays, I've only seen *More Stately Mansions* which was too long. Even though the cast spoke simultaneously and as fast as they could, it still went on for three and a half hours. You know you're in for it with Mr. Spacey and I'm sure he did a hell of a job.

Nevertheless, I'm convinced that theatre, like life, has lost its sense of poetry. I saw a play recently by Mr. Albee[96] called *Three Tall Women,* but even that hadn't really anything to move you. It's not that theatre is superficial, it's that it doesn't contain anything that you can take away and enjoy outside of what is going on the stage. It's not that it's shallow, it's that it's expressed in a way that makes it more ordinary instead of uplifting.

I don't see many plays because they are so expensive. The other night, I went to see *The Mystery of Irma Vep*[97] which was great fun. It's a wild farce with everyone rushing in and out and changing their costume, making faces and so on. It must

---

94 Kevin Spacey, American actor and director, b. 1959
95 A play written by Eugene O'Neill, American playwright and Nobel laureate in Literature, 1888-1953
96 Edward Albee, American playwright, 1928-2016
97 By Charles Ludlam, American actor, director, and playwright, 1943-1987

have been very well rehearsed because it took place on a very small stage and they only fell on the floor when they were meant to. It was so overloaded with meaning that you couldn't really get it all, but it was very funny and very entertaining. It wasn't on Broadway though, it was in the Westside Theatre, a small theatre on 43rd Street.

Of all that's on in the big theatres, I have only seen *Sunset Boulevard* which I thought was entertaining. The pity about *Sunset Boulevard*, of course, is that the musical's best song occurs within the first twenty minutes of the show and nothing else quite equals it. I remember Ms. Paige[98] shooting her boyfriend. Three times. Once as he stands in front of her, once as he goes down the steps and once when he comes to the edge of the stage and falls in to the orchestra pit. We know it to be the swimming pool because we've all seen the movie, which by the way was better than the play. I spoke to Ms. Paige after the performance and said to her, "Shouldn't the young man take his curtain calls wringing wet?"

She didn't agree. She thought this would be taking realism too far. Personally, I don't think you can take anything too far on the stage.

Perhaps one day I will have my own name in lights on Broadway. Not for my one-man show, of course, I would never be able to fill the theatre, but for my very own musical. You see, I know a famous composer called Mr. Adler.[99] He's a very serious composer. Nevertheless, he has set some of my

---

98 Elaine Paige, English singer and actress, b. 1948
99 James Adler, American pianist and composer, b. 1950

poems to music so I think there is a chance I can convert him to jollity.

My plan is to write with him a musical version of Tarzan, called "My Man, Tarzan" because Tarzan is the great American myth. I have planned it all. There will even be a chorus of pygmies, who will sing, "Do you dig me, Mrs. Pygmy?" Various songs are already planned. I don't think anything really has to happen plot-wise, so long as the whole thing takes place in the jungle. Jane comes along and meets Tarzan. The real Lord Greystoke appears because he's in the book[100] and he sings a song which says, "Is he a decent chap? If ever we get back to a smart racetrack, will he wear a topper like your papa, or will he wear a palm leaf cap? Will he do a handstand in the grandstand? Is he a decent chap?"

In the book, of course, Jane does not stay in the jungle. She goes back to Maryland. My musical will have a song where she sings, "I dream of my fairyland, Maryland, home." In my version she will stay in the jungle and she and Tarzan will be lovers and everyone will be happy.

I did start writing an opera once when I lived in London. It was the Trojan legend from the point of view of Cassandra who as you know was a vestal virgin. When the Spartans came to Troy, she went to the Temple of Minerva and she prayed, but it was to no avail. She was raped by Ajax and of course, it was the insult to Minerva that frightened Agamemnon.

I wrote a lot of the opera and then Mr. Bridemore,[101] the composer with whom I wished to work, read what I had

---

100 By Edgar Rice Burroughs, American writer, 1875-1950
101 It's unclear who Quentin was working with

written and said to me, "There seems to be a lot of standing about in your opera."

To which I explained, "It's all standing about."

And he said, "I don't want that." Which made no sense to me.

To me, all opera singers do is stand about. You can't sing like that and *do* anything.

There is a singer[102] in America who wears horn-rimmed spectacles and stands almost perfectly still when she performs. A man who was with me when I saw her on my television set said, "I can't stand people like that. They don't do anything for the numbers."

I corrected him. "Yes, they do." I said, "They sing them." You can't sing and jump up and down and break your guitar. You can only shout and do that.

I should think I left the manuscript for my great Trojan musical in a drawer in Beaufort Street. I imagine it was subsequently destroyed when someone took over my room. It's probably for the best. There's quite enough rubbish on Broadway these days as it is.

---

102 Lisa Loeb, American singer, b. 1968

CHAPTER 11

My So-called Career

MR. WARHOL,[103] WHOM I BUMPED into from time to time at the various events we both attended in the eighties, famously said, "In the future, everyone will be famous for fifteen minutes." I have news for you. With luck, or effort, you can extend those fifteen minutes quite considerably. Even if you are as old and hopelessly untalented as I am.

In fact, everything I say on stage during my one-man show is to help people extend their fifteen minutes so that it might become a wonderful lifetime. This, of course, assumes that the people seeing my show want to be famous. I'm sure there are some people in the world who don't but I seldom meet one of them.

You see, I have lied to you. Not a hurtful lie, but a lie nonetheless. When I talk about how I have never worked and how I have never had a career, I am, of course, negating my so-called career as a celebrity. The reason I don't really think of it as a career is because it's been so unpredictable. If I were to write a

---

103 Andy Warhol, American pop artist, director and producer, 1928-1987

resume for myself, it would be a horrible mess. For in my time I have been an author, I have appeared on stage, I have written for newspapers and magazines, I have been on television, I have been in films, I have made voice recordings, I have posed for photographs and paintings and I have sung for my supper almost as many times as I have eaten.

Looking back, I suppose I have to call all of that a career although it never afforded me any kind of security. I never had any colleagues or a workplace that I had to attend. But as a whole I suppose it's not unimpressive. I know plenty of aspiring actors who would saw off a leg or an arm for the opportunities that have been presented to me. So, it is with the greatest respect to them that I want to walk you through some of the highlights of my so-called career.

I am not really an actor, but over the years I have appeared in various shows. I have never trained as an actor. I never go to auditions and do all those things that aspiring actors do. I only get into movies by mistake. So, I feel free to criticize them. If you want to live in New York and not appear in films, you have to keep moving because the moment you stand still someone comes up and says, "Would you like to be in our movie?" Of course, I never say no to anything. So frequently, I say yes. As a result I have been in the most extraordinary movies.

The Bride[104] was the first movie I appeared in and I must say how interesting it was to see from the inside just how a

---

104 1985, directed by Franc Roddam, English film director, b. 1946

film is made. Nobody speaks unless they are wearing a microphone. As such, actors whisper to one another in a windowless room brimming with other people. I didn't realize that movie sets were so quiet. It took me quite a while to get used to that. I didn't have many lines. Come to think of it, I might not have had any at all.

Mr. Sting[105] was nice. He played the role of Dr. Frankenstein, since *The Bride* was a remake of the eponymous legend. He has not had good luck with his films. First of all he was in *Quadrophenia*.[106] Then he was in *The Bride* which the critics hated. Then he had a tiny part in *Plenty*,[107] alongside Ms. Streep,[108] which people overlooked. Then he was in something else, but he's never had a hit. He even played Mack The Knife on Broadway[109] which I would have thought he was ideally cast for, but the show closed after a few weeks and got very poor reviews. I think the people who went to see him wanted to hear him sing more than act.

One of the things that intrigued me about being on set were the efforts to ensure continuity. What did they do before there was instant photography? Every evening, just as the director said, "Cut. That's it." We would all rise up and then someone would shout, "Stay a moment." And we would all sit down again. Then they would take photographs of the set so that

---

105 Or just simply Sting – see footnote #31
106 Directed by Franc Roddam, 1979
107 Directed by Fred Schepisi, 1985
108 Meryl Streep, award-winning American actress, b. 1949
109 In 1989, in Bertolt Brecht and Kurt Weill's *Threepenny Opera*

they could put everything back just the way it was and so that everyone in the scene could look exactly the same when filming resumed the next day or possibly later. Before instant photography, I imagine some poor girl having to write down a description of what everyone was wearing, where they stood and what was in the background. Something like "Two books on the second shelf, there are flowers on the side table..."

The first American movie I was in was *Aunt Fannie*[110] in which I played the title role. Unfortunately my character dies before the film begins. It was the first film I made with Mr. Needleman.[111] Afterwards I made *Red Ribbons*[112] although I only had a tiny part.

In *Red Ribbons* I played a guest at a wake for a man who was gay and had died. The movie is based on the plot of a French novel whose title can be translated as *The Revelation* in which a woman's son dies and she looks through his possessions and finds and reads a bundle of his letters. They are love letters from a man and she has to get used to this.

In our film, a woman, Mrs. Niles, reads her son's letters and then comes to a wake held for her son by his dubious friends of whom I am one. My character's name was Horace Nightingale III. Most of the film takes place with us all sitting around in a room in an apartment on Flatbush Avenue, Brooklyn. I don't know why we filmed it there. The room we used was as non-descript as any other. It was small and consequently became

---

110 Directed by Neil Needleman, released on video in 1994
111 Neil Ira Needleman, video artist and video-maker, b. 1957
112 Directed by Neil Needleman, also released on video in 1994

very crowded. The apartment belonged to a man who had said he would allow us to use it, if in return he was allowed to meet the actress playing Mrs. Niles. It turned out that Ms. Spelvin,[113] who played Mrs. Niles, used to appear in adult films before retiring in the early eighties. Despite appearing in his movies, I don't hear from Mr. Needleman anymore. I should think he has read the reviews for his films in the newspapers and given up filmmaking.

Later, I was in a film called *Barriers*[114] in which I was a delicatessen owner who gets gunned down in the first few minutes of the film. I was shot by a black man walking through my shop. I don't think you see me fall to the ground, but I think you hear the shots. That was a very strange movie.

Then I appeared, or rather I should say I narrated, a short movie that was a black-and-white film about *Little Red Riding Hood*.[115] I confess, I've never seen it so I have no idea what it's like. They showed me just enough for me to fit my voice to it.

The role for which I've received the most praise however, was when I played Queen Elizabeth I in the 1993 film *Orlando*.[116] My involvement was Ms. Potter's[117] idea. She came to New York, I hope not just to see me, but she saw me and asked if I would read some lines for her. So I read them and

---

113 Georgina Spelvin, born Michelle Graham, b. 1936

114 Directed by Alan Baxter, 1998

115 *Little Red Riding Hood and Other Stories.* Directed by David Kaplan, 1997, also starring Christina Ricci.

116 Directed by Sally Potter, 1992, starring Tilda Swanton and Billy Zane.

117 Sally Potter, English film director and screenwriter, b. 1949

she asked me, "Will you play the part?" And, of course, I never say no to anything.

Nevertheless, I have to confess that filming *Orlando* was absolute hell because I wore a bodice so tight that it blistered my stomach. I had two rolls of fabric tied around my middle with tapes, so I always had to sit forward. Then I wore a taut skirt, a quilted petticoat, an ordinary petticoat and a dress over all of that. Once dressed, I couldn't make it out of the trailer in which all of these things were put on me without someone lifting up the whole lot and giving me directions. They would say, "Put your foot down. Further. Now the other one. More. Now you're on level ground." I never saw my feet during the whole production. Then, of course, I had to heave all that taffeta over the grounds of Hatfield House.[118]

Luckily, it only took two weeks for me to finish my part in the film, so really the whole thing was remarkably easy and Ms. Potter was a very good director. When things had to be done again she would say so and tell you exactly why. She never nagged and she never made any unkind comments. In fact, nothing that I expected would happen on a movie set ever took place. Nobody burst into tears, nobody ran off the set and nobody slapped someone else's face. It all passed in a very calm, civilized way.

People always ask how I prepared for playing Queen Elizabeth I in *Orlando* and I never know how to reply.

---

118 A palace in England, built in 1497, childhood home of Queen Elizabeth I.

Obviously they expect me to say that I had some ritual or method, but the truth is I didn't prepare at all. I don't really know what people mean when they say 'prepare'. When required to, I simply said the words as though I meant them. I didn't try to think myself into the part or what it would be like to have lived in those times and to have ruled over England.

For all I know, Queen Elizabeth I may have spoken English in quite a different way from how we do now, but I didn't bother with any of that. For me, acting is more innate. It's true, there's all this business in America about learning how to act, but I can't see what it means. If an actor asked me, "How should I prepare myself to play a part?" I would answer, "Don't prepare yourself. You've been chosen by the director because he thinks you are like the person he has in mind. All you have to do is be yourself and say the lines as though you mean them, as though they were you own." It worked for me and the only thing I can do well, the only thing I know how to do, is be *me*.

Many people consider my portrayal of Queen Elizabeth I to be the perfect queen. That's very nice of them. My personal opinion is that Ms. Blanchett[119] who played the same role in *Elizabeth*[120] was better. She certainly looked much more like the portraits that were made of England's Virgin Queen during her lifetime with her long, beautiful, triangular face and her exquisite pallor. In contrast, I don't think Ms. Dench was

---

119 Cate Blanchett, Australian actress and director, b. 1969
120 Directed by Shekhar Kapur, 1998

anything like Queen Elizabeth. Even though they gave her an Oscar for the role.[121]

For the 1998 film *Homo Heights,*[122] I travelled to Minneapolis at the request of Ms. Moore.[123] the film's writer and director. She once worked as a clown. Now she's a movie director. That's America for you. Anyway she invited me to play the role of Malcolm.

Homo Heights was the name given to a fictitious district of Minneapolis where the movie's principal gay people are supposed to live. In the film, it is ruled by a drag queen called Maria Callous who runs a nightclub called Tosca. She is a despot and tells everyone what to do. Mr. Sorrentino[124] played the drag queen and was wonderful. I've seen the finished film and he is very, very funny.

As well as being an actor, Mr. Sorrentino is a famous impressionist. He imitates Elton John in a show in Las Vegas so successfully that he has bought a house in Las Vegas. I imagine he must be very well paid. In *Homo Heights,* I play his ex-lover, his slave and his tormentor, all wrapped up in one person. Ultimately I escape to outer space. That's basically the storyline. Every day, Mr. Sorrentino would walk around the set laughing and saying, "I hope my father never sees this film."

I actually saw *Homo Heights* at the Archives[125] yesterday with my great nephew. When you see it, you can hardly follow

---

121 For Best Supporting Actress in 1998's *Shakespeare in Love.*

122 Released 1998

123 Sara Moore, actress and director.

124 Stephen Sorrentino, actor and impersonator b. 1960

125 Anthology Film Archives, home of experimental cinema in New York City.

the plot. I first saw it at a screening at the Angelica Theater when it was first released. I saw it again and again and each time I did it seemed more obscure, not clearer. Ms. Moore was not there yesterday because she is apparently busy being a clown in a circus in California. Afterwards, we went to The Bowery Bar with Ms. Lehman[126] who was the producer, and another younger woman who had worked on the film and was there with her boyfriend.

I've made several more movies but I can't remember all their names. None of them can ever be seen. They go straight into video stores. I have never understood videos. They cost $40 dollars. And the video is in a sealed box which you cannot open. So you end up paying $40 for something which you don't know anything about, what it's like or if it's any good. Anyway, that's what happened with most of my movies.

If another movie of my life were being filmed today, I don't know who should portray me. Mr. Hurt[127] of course, is now fifty, so it might be difficult for him. He was younger when they originally filmed *The Naked Civil Servant.*[128] Everyone's very self-conscious about playing homosexual parts though. I never know why. When anyone takes a homosexual part, the press asks, "Have you discussed this with your wife and children?" And the actor always says, "Oh, yes. They're completely behind me." If you played the part of a priest or a disgraced

126 Kate Lehman, executive producer
127 Sir John Vincent Hurt, English actor, 1940-2017
128 Directed by Jack Gold, 1975

politician last week, why should it matter if you play a homosexual this week? The whole thing baffles me.

In addition to starring in films, I've also been lucky enough to be paid to appear in commercials. And the great thing about appearing in commercials is you go on getting paid for them long after you've finished filming them, just so long as they're still being aired.

People always complain about all the waiting around required for film and TV work, but of course I spent the majority of my early life as a model. All I ever did was sit or stand around waiting, so it makes no difference to me. When asked about the downtime involved in movie making Mr. Mitchum[129] said, "It beats working, any day." And it does.

The first commercial I did was for Mr. Klein[130] and was for a perfume called ck one[131] which was said to be suitable for men as well as women. They organized a car to take me to the location where we would be shooting and I remember a limousine drawing up in front of the house, which was as long as the block. Sheepishly, I got into it. The car was so large though, that when it turned the street corner, I fell onto the floor. I quickly got up again. I don't think the driver saw.

As the limousine's windows were darkened, I can't tell you exactly where we went, but I think we went to Queens. Anyway, when I got out of the car, I found myself in a space

---

129 Robert Mitchum, American film actor and director, 1917-1997
130 Calvin Klein, American fashion designer, b. 1942
131 The campaign aired in 1995

so big it was like an airplane hangar. I thought to myself, "We could film the charge of the light brigade in here."

Standing on a piece of paper about six feet long and two feet wide were six very thin people, so I went and stood with them. While I stood there engaging in conversation, a man, naked to the waist, crawled on the floor between our feet. I turned and said to Mr. Klein, "What does it all mean?" Mr. Klein's eyes flashed and he smiled and said, "Say that again." And by mistake, I had written the copy. That's all the advertisement said. "ck one. What does it all mean?" The experience was a little frightening, but it was fun and I did enjoy doing it. I later found out that one of the very thin people was a young lady called Kate Moss.[132]

The next commercial I did was for Levi Strauss jeans.[133] In it I appear at the table of a kind of speakeasy club, talking with other elderly men and women. At one point I was asked about nothing in particular and I responded with the line, "An intriguing mix." I think I'm the only person in the advert who is not wearing Levis, but this you can't tell because I am seated at a table when the camera zooms in on me.

For my third commercial, I was flown to Miami, Florida. It was for another perfume, this time for Faberge's Impulse[134] body spray. The title of the commercial was 'Encounter' and the advert featured two men stopping to help a girl who has

---

132 Kate Moss, English model, b. 1974

133 The campaign aired from 1997-1998, containing six separate commercials and was titled 'They Go On'.

134 For a campaign that aired in 1998

dropped her bag of groceries. As one of the men helps collect her fruit and vegetables from the floor, he smells her and almost falls in love with her. His friend snaps him out of his trance and the two of them walk off. Confused, the girl looks around her and sees a number of gay stereotypes and situations, one of them being a quizzical me standing on a nearby street corner, whereupon she realizes that the only reason she didn't snag her man is because he's gay. We are thus left to assume that the man's friend was, in fact, his boyfriend.

I thought it was a very brave commercial given the overtly gay theme, but of course, it was an advertisement principally aimed at young women. When I arrived on location, because we shot the commercial on a real life street, one of the production crew immediately brought a wig for me to wear. Obviously, they weren't happy with the state of my own hair. They also provided me with a straw hat, which was much more in keeping with the local weather and which I also wore.

The only other commercial I've ever done was for West cigarettes. That was a print commercial though, not one for television. I was flown to Hollywood and put up in the Mondrian Hotel which was very grand. I was taken out into the street and offered a wooden cigarette by a wooden actor. Now I've never smoked and I said to the people taking the photographs, "This is absurd. I don't smoke and I've never smoked."

One of the men replied, "The absurdity is the point. Before we photographed you, we photographed a mermaid blessing one of the cigarettes."

It makes about as much sense to me now as it did then.

Now, when I first came to New York, they didn't have the recorded voices you now hear in taxis telling you to wear a seatbelt. Then one day they all of a sudden appeared. Anyway, one day I was whizzing down Second Avenue in a cab when I heard the voice of Eartha Kitt say, "A cat has nine lives, but you have only one..."

And I thought this was so wonderful I decided that I would like to speak in a taxi myself. I decided I would say, "Life, to be sure, is not that much to lose, but if you think it is, buckle your seatbelt."

I eventually recorded my voiceover, but I don't know if they ever used it. I haven't yet gotten into a taxi and heard my own voice speaking to me. I suppose the message would be more poignant if they used it when I'm no longer around. Assuming anyone remembers who I am. Otherwise they'll just sit there wondering whose voice they just heard.

CHAPTER 12

My One-man Show

I WAS PUT ON THE stage by my English agent[135] who was Hungarian. And you never understand why Hungarians do or say the things they do. He had taken a theatre about the size of a living room behind a public house in Islington[136] where he was putting on a show directed by a woman in whom he was interested. There were opening hours in those days which meant the theatre had two practical slots. A lunchtime slot and an evening slot. He already knew what he was doing with the evening hours.

So he said to me in his dreamy Hungarian voice, "I don't want to waste the lunchtime hours. I thought you could go on then."

And I said, "With what object?"

And he said, "You could talk to people." When I asked about what, he said, "It doesn't matter. You needn't say the same thing each day, if you don't want to."

---

135 Richard Gollner, who became Quentin's agent when Donald Carroll, 1940-2010, returned to the U.S.
136 The Kings Head Theatre

So I went on the stage and I spoke. Then I spoke some more. Frequently we were down to three people and when that was the case I would get down from the stage and sit with them and chat. It was more intimate that way.

Once the television show[137] of my life had been aired it all changed. The theatre was suddenly filled with people. In fact, we literally went from an audience of three to a full house of around a hundred, overnight. The Hungarian was pleased.

A witness to my modest success was a tall man by the name of Mr. Jackson[138] who took up my cause and put me on at The Mayfair Theatre. It was still a tiny little theatre but its audience capacity was twice that of the King's Head.

Mr. Jackson seemed to live in an ivory tower in Knightsbridge from which he could survey the whole of London's West End theatre district. Whenever he saw the lights go out in a theatre, he would run all the way there and say, "I can find you someone who will appear at any moment with no rehearsals and no lighting."

He was referring, of course, to me. On one such occasion, and at great surprise to me, someone actually took him up on his offer.

A Mr. Rix[139] was the manager of the Duke of York's Theatre at the time when his theatre was hosting a play that I think was called *The Spy Chiller.* Anyway, it did so badly that, night

---

137 1975's *The Naked Civil Servant*, directed by Jack Gold
138 Possibly the manager of The Mayfair Theatre
139 Brian Norman Roger Rix, actor, activist and one-time producer at Cooney-Marsh Ltd. which owned the Duke of York's Theatre, 1924-2016

after night, there were more people on the stage than in the audience. So it was taken off. Mr. Rix needed a stopgap before he could get another big production in, otherwise he would lose more than 2,500 pounds a week.

At the suggestion of Mr. Jackson, I went to see Mr. Rix and he agreed to let me take up a temporary residence at his theatre. Then, when I was already on the stage, Equity[140] came marching down St. Martin's Lane with its ragged banners and a furious Ms. Redgrave[141] at the head of a mob. She challenged Mr. Rix, asking him, "Why is Mr. Crisp acting in a West End theatre without an Equity card?"

To which Mr. Rix who was never at a loss for words, replied, "Mr. Crisp is not acting. He's very sincere."

This, however, was thought to be a specious argument and I was made to have an Equity card.[142]

When I look back though, it's quite remarkable. I was in a West End theatre without any experience at all of being on the stage. I never understood it. At one point, during the question and answer part of my show, I was asked, "Did Doctor Livingston have style?"

To which I answered, "He did."

Then the follow-up asked, "Was going to Africa part of his style?"

And I said, "It was his whole style."

---

140 The British trade union for actors
141 Vanessa Redgrave, English actress and political activist, b. 1937
142 Equivalent to union membership

And the audience roared with laughter. I never knew why. If you say what you think, everybody laughs. If you try to make jokes, nobody laughs.

Once my four weeks were up at The Duke of York's Theatre, I found myself appearing at The Ambassador's Theatre which had been the theatre where *The Mousetrap*[143] was first shown. When I left on the final night the stage doorman said to me, "You're going? I thought you could have been a one-man *Mousetrap*."

I smiled at his kind remark. The only time I've ever been on the stage in the West End was on those two occasions.

The audience for my one-man show now is different from when I first did it in 1978. It's better now. More people come and more mention is made of it in the paper, but I am no better at it. I always think people will eventually rise up and say, "We've had it. Don't let him do it again." But thankfully they have yet to do so.

When I tour, I typically go to the same places. Mr. Lago arranges performances for me in places like Los Angeles and San Diego. I always expect the audience to say, "We've heard it all. He's done all this before. We know all the jokes." But it seems there are always enough people in the world to keep the audience going. This I find surprising, but very nice. Strangers are, after all, my bread and butter.

I was recently asked if I have ever been asked a question to which I was startled. The only question of this vein that

---

143 A play by Agatha Christie that has been running in London since 1952.

sticks out in my mind was when a man once asked me if I'd ever milked a cow. He was pleased with that. You see, people want the questions to be part of the entertainment. You can't prevent them doing that because that's what you get when you invite the audience to participate in the show. They want to be part of the entertainment. That's why they make the questions funny.

I like it, but of course, it's not really why they are invited to ask questions. They're asked so that I can say the words they wish to hear. Some, of course, do. And I never tire of having the same questions asked because I like knowing the answers and being able to rattle them off while thinking of something else.

I've memorized the lines of my one-man show through sheer repetition. I constantly forgot them in the beginning. I didn't dry up, or die on stage as I think it's called. Instead I would turn to the audience and say, "What shall we talk about now?"

But after about five or six weeks of saying it every night, I got used to it. So, I've learnt it from perpetual reiteration. Until recently my show didn't even have a script, any direction or any rehearsals. My theory was that every show's rehearsal was the show that came before it.

Now there is a script because we have typed out what I have to say. I have read through it and I now know it by heart. Having an actual script is a great help. If I've not done the show for eighteen months, I can read through the script as though it were a very posh magazine and remind myself how it goes.

I don't dread my stage show in any way. I just go and do it. I don't really question it. I don't say, "Why am I doing all this? Why don't I just sit at home?" I did feel that about being a model. I used to think, "I've got to get up and go to Guilford, which means going to Waterloo and catching a train. Then, when I arrive in Guilford I have to walk from the station to the art school, all in order to earn a pound and come back home again." But when I work in the theatre, it's more or less effortless.

And after performing my show, I always go home and go to bed. A lot of actors - I am *not* an actor so I should instead say a lot of performers - say they have to wind down after a show. I assume this means they really work themselves up to appear on stage, hence the need to calm down again afterwards. Sometimes I think I should work myself up to appear on stage, but I never do. Being on the stage is exactly the same for me as being anywhere else.

While I was at the Duke of York's a Mr. Elkins[144] came to see me and asked if I would consent to take my show to America. To which I said, "I want what you want," which is what I said to everything.

"In that case," he replied back, "we shall never quarrel."

And we never did.

I went to New York where I stayed at the Algonquin Hotel. It was not the first time I'd been to America. I first came to America in 1977 when I came and stayed at the Drake Hotel at the invitation of Mr. Bennett[145] who wanted to make *The Naked Civil Servant* into a musical. This I would have

---

144 Hillard Elkins, Producer, 1929-2010.

145 Michael Bennett, American musical theatre director, writer, choreographer, and dancer, 1943-1987

loved, but my agent eventually said it was not to be. I never knew why.

My adventure with Mr. Elkins began the year after in December 1978. I performed my show in a theatre on MacDougal Street called The Player's Theatre. The Player's is a very nice and small theatre and everyone that worked there was very kind to me. My run lasted for three months.

Once we had closed in New York, Mr. Elkins had arranged for me to perform for three months in Los Angeles. My run there started most auspiciously with an opening night at the Ahmanson Theatre to please a man called Mr. Ward. I don't know why he wanted me to be in the Ahmanson, but when I saw it, tears began to fall from my eyes because it was the size of a cathedral.

They said, "You'll be wired for sound."

So I had to tell them, "I cannot stand at a microphone. I have to pace up and down."

And they said, "That'll be all right."

This confused me so I clarified, "I also cannot hold a microphone in my hand as I have to use my hands."

They reassured me, "You'll be able to."

Then they filled my pockets with little vulcanite boxes and when I spoke, my voice boomed all over the building. It was magical.

There was a Los Angeles critic at the time called Sylvia Drake and I remember she gave me a wonderful notice which began, "Where were you on Sunday evening?" Anyway, I believe it was her praise that led to my receiving a Drama

Critic's Circle Award for my one-man show. So, after travelling up to San Francisco to debut my show at the Lillian Memorial Theatre for a few weeks, I returned to Los Angeles to pick up my award.

Picking up my award wasn't the only reason I was excited to be back in L.A. I had learned that Ms. Harris[146] would be present at the awards ceremony and I longed to meet her. When we got into the hall where the ceremony was taking place, I asked Mr. Elkins, "Is she here?" And he looked around the huge hall and in the distance he saw a little woman in a black dress sitting by herself at her table.

He threaded his way through the tables until he came to Ms. Harris, then asked if might he bring me to meet her. Instead of that, she rose and came across the whole floor to meet me. It was the essence of noblesse oblige. It was I who should have walked over and bowed to her. She had style and it was vintage Hollywood down to the core.

Ms. Harris was in a stage production of *On Golden Pond*[147] in which she acted with a wonderful actor called Mr. Durning[148] who had himself been marvelous playing opposite Ms. Stapleton[149] in the film *Queen of the Stardust Ballroom*[150].

I got to know her niece, also called Julie, who later[151] took me to see a one-woman show Ms. Harris performed in New

146 Julie Harris, five-time Tony-award winning American actress, 1925-2013
147 A 1979 play by Ernest Thompson, later a film.
148 Charles Durning, American actor, 1923-2012
149 Maureen Stapleton, American actress, 1925-2006
150 Directed by Sam O'Steen, 1975
151 In 1991

York called *Lucifer's Child*.[152] Afterwards, we all went to the Russian Tea Room to have dinner. As we arrived, I held back the door so that Ms. Harris could make a grand entrance. This she did not do. She crept into the restaurant as though she were an ordinary mortal, which both disappointed and pleasantly surprised me at the same time.

From there I went back to England, and then I thought, "I can't live without it. I must go back to America." So, I packed up my belongings in a little red handkerchief and tied them to the end of a stick and put them up there on my shoulder and came to America. Now New York is my home. I hope never to be deported. If I am, I shall live in Canada and tiptoe across the undefended parallel.

When I first appeared on stage, I remember standing in the wings with my hands above my head, so that my hands would be pale and the veins would have disappeared when I got onto the stage. That's what I'd read all chorus girls do. I also shut my eyes so that when I opened them they were dark and wet. Afterwards I would breathe deeply through my nose so as to take up the slack in your stomach, and then bring it out. That was to get my engine going. My makeup is always by me. I think nearly all artists do their own makeup. Particularly Ms. Collins[153] who knows just how to look like Joan Collins. I mean, she's looked the same way for fifty years.

My voice is very flat and I wish it were richer and rounder and more beautiful, but of course, I didn't know I was going

---

152 A play by William Luce, American writer, b. 1931
153 Joan Collins, English actress, b. 1933

to be put into the public speaking racket when I began, or I else would have had something done about it. I can usually reach an audience. I never had a microphone in England even when I was at the Duke of York's. Though when they opened the gallery on Saturdays, I was saddened to hear I couldn't always be heard by the patrons sitting up there.

I don't know if I have any stage presence. I certainly try. I try to enter very slowly, this somehow allows you take in your audience without doing anything or saying anything. There are certain people who occupy the stage when they come on. Mr. Pavarotti had it. Ms. Bankhead[154] had it too. She arrived on stage and everyone of course went mad and screamed and shrieked and clapped. She looked as though she enjoyed it, that she was grateful, and that she was at your service in some way. That's what you try to do. If you're not careful though you do it when you enter rooms, which of course is a sin.

Other than for my one-man show, the only other time I've been on stage was when I played Lady Bracknell in the *Importance of Being Earnest*[155] on a small stage where I could be heard simply by raising my voice. It was a production in a dim cellar on Mercer Street, and I was offered the part having only been in America for about eighteen months.

It wasn't a pleasant experience because it took place during a very hot August in a theatre with no air conditioning. All you could hear was the fluttering of programs throughout the

---

154 Tallulah Bankhead, American actress, 1902-1968
155 By Oscar Wilde – see footnote #77

show as people wafted them about, trying to keep cool. I, of course, was dressed up like a dog's dinner.

It was actually the first and only play I've acted in since I was a child. Playing Lady Bracknell is a very easy part because it's short and showy. You can hardly do it wrong. Her lines are funny on their own so you don't have to point them out or make them funny. They just are. These days I couldn't be in another play because I would never be able to remember the lines.

CHAPTER 13

The Naked Civil Servant

THE NAKED CIVIL SERVANT[156] MAY have been the most successful book I've ever written but it wasn't the first book I had written. There were others. Chiefly these were handbooks on lettering or window dressing. *The Naked Civil Servant* was the first book of mine to cause any kind of stir however.

I did write a satire called *All This And Bevin Too*[157] when Mr. Bevin[158] was the Minister of Labor in England. It was a continuous limerick about an unemployed kangaroo, but it was a thin little book with a paper cover that caused no sensation whatsoever.

The people who caused me to write *The Naked Civil Servant*, the story of my life, can be said to have been the greatest influences in my life. It was Mr. O'Connor's[159] radio interview with me for the BBC's[160] *Third Programme*[161] that

---

156 First published in 1968

157 Published in 1943

158 Ernest Bevin, British politician, 1881-1951

159 Philip O'Connor, English writer and radio host, 1916-1998

160 The British Broadcasting Corporation

161 A national radio service broadcast by the BBC that started in September 1946 and was eventually absorbed into Radio 3 in 1970.

started it all. I was one of a series of hooligans Mr. O'Conner interviewed. He knew a lot of us because he himself was a regular visitor to Fitzrovia back in the 1930s.

Then, as luck would have it, a literary agent by the name of Mr. Carroll heard my interview with Mr. O'Connor and suggested I write a book about my life experiences and philosophy. I had originally wanted to call the book *I Reign In Hell*, referencing Milton's[162] line in *Paradise Lost*[163] but Mr. Carroll was having none of it. Though he was a Milton fan, he thought the reference[164] too obscure, the word 'reign' too pretentious and believed having the world 'Hell' in the title would scare people away. He thought *The Naked Civil Servant* was a much more intriguing title and that, I am glad to say, is what we went with.

The publication of *The Naked Civil Servant* by Jonathon Cape Ltd.[165] did not mark a huge turning point in my life however. Nowadays, historians say the book was a bestseller at the time. It was no such thing. It sold its edition which if memory serves was about three thousand copies, but that was not enough to make it a bestseller. Had it sold thirty thousand it would still not have been a bestseller. It would have taken sales of more like three hundred thousand in order to be a bestseller. What publication did however, was slowly get the ball rolling.

---

162 John Milton, English poet, 1608-1674
163 Milton's most famous work, first published in 1667
164 'Better to reign in Hell, than serve in Heav'n', Line 263
165 Founded in 1921 and nowadays part of the Random House Group

Reviews for *The Naked Civil Servant* weren't altogether bad and sales were further helped by a documentary about me that was made by the talented Mr. Mitchell[166] for Granada Television.[167] It was this broadcast that was seen by my friend Mr. Haggerty and which sparked an idea in his head for a film.

Mr. Haggerty introduced me to a man called Mr. Mackie[168] whom I helped write a screenplay based on my book. Our original idea was to turn it into a movie, but we had trouble getting interest from film studios despite an early interest and commitment from Mr. Hurt to play the role of me.

Eventually Thames Television picked up *The Naked Civil Servant* and the rest, as they say, is history. Mr. Haggerty imagined it, Mr. Mackie wrote it, Ms. Lambert produced it, Mr. Gold[169] directed it and Mr. Hurt played the lead role. I am incredibly indebted to these people because they were the way in which I came not just to America, but the way in which I came before the public. After *The Naked Civil Servant* was broadcast in England[170] and later in America,[171] Mr. Hurt became my official representative here on Earth.

But, as I stated at the beginning of this chapter, *The Naked Civil Servant* was not the first book I had written. It was my

---

166 Denis Mitchell, British documentary filmmaker, 1911-1990

167 Originally broadcast in 1969 and then again in 1970 as part of the *World In Action* series.

168 Philip Mackie, English writer and producer, 1918–1985

169 Jack Gold, English director and producer, 1930–2015

170 On 17th December, 1975

171 In 1976

fourth. My first two books, one on calligraphy[172] and another on window dressing,[173] were written more than thirty years before when I was in my late twenties.

At the time, I worked in the art department of a printer who printed the handbooks put out by the Blanford Press which wrote books about sign writing, window display and everything else connected with pictorial advertising. Blanford Press were based on Blanford Street which was a turning off of Baker Street in London. They paid me to write both books and because of this I've only ever written the books I was told to write. I've never sat in my room thinking, "I will write a book," because I wouldn't have the self-assurance.

As a graphic artist, I created book covers, but I don't remember all the book covers that I did. I can remember a book called *Freemasons' Guide and Compendium*[174] for which I did a cover. I think it contained a T-square and a pair of dividers that I arranged in a pattern. I did the less important books as well as the ones that sold principally on their covers like romances, thrillers and westerns.

You see, the latter of these book types sold on the book-stands in mainline railway stations. While waiting for their train, a passenger will say, "I'd better have something to read on my journey." Then they see a book with a gun on it with fire coming out of the end of it, which of course never happens, and they think, "That looks like a good read." Or else

---

172 *Lettering for Brush and Pen*, 1936, published by Stuart, Frederick Warne Ltd.
173 *Colour in Display*, 1938, published by The Blandford Press
174 By Bernard E Jones, published 1950

they see a darkened cover and a torch focused on some false teeth lying on the ground and they think, "Oh, that looks exciting. I'll buy that." Or they see a girl with red hair with her shoulder strap broken being lifted up in the arms of a man and they think, "Oh, how romantic. I shall buy that."

In order to create an effective cover, you need to know what kind of a person would buy the book you're designing for. You rapidly learn to skim through a book rather than to read it to see what kind of person the story is intended for.

If you're flicking through and the author says, "Her eyes filled with tears and her breasts rose and fell," you know it's for men. This would require a cover featuring a woman with long, wavy red hair. Had the book been written for a female market it would have said, "Her eyes filled with tears and her *bosom* rose and fell," this would necessitate a cover featuring a dark-haired woman. If the book hadn't mentioned the crying woman's breasts at all, it would be for children. In this case you draw a cover with a woman with straight, short, muted blonde hair. Those are the basic rules of how you do covers for books.

A Barbara Cartland novel would of course require a romantic proposition. As such, an embracing couple in eighteenth century costume might be appropriate with the man always taller than the woman. The woman might be leaning on his chest and looking up at him and he would be looking down at her. He would be clean-shaven, with clear, cleft features and probably be in uniform.

In *Colour in Display* I endeavored to suggest chiefly that if you are dressing a window it must have a prevailing color. You can't have a window dressed in red, blue, and green because it doesn't work. You have to have a window which, from a long way off, you can see is a blue window. That way passersby think, "I wonder what it's like." Then they come and look at it. I also impressed upon my readers, not that there would have been very many, that you should never make your displays more spectacular than the thing or things you are displaying.

I also said that the maximum point of interest lies in the maximum point of contrast and that the greatest contrast is not between black and white but between black and yellow. This is because black and white are contrasted in color, but not in glow. Yellow, on the other hand, is a vibrant color while black is a negative color. That's why the contrast between the two is the greatest there is.

I explained that window displays need a contrast in size. This means that the ideal display contains a little bit of yellow and a black background. That attracts everybody. I arrived at all this purely by thinking about it. I wrote it all up and made it a book for which I was paid sixty pounds. That was a lot of money for me back then.

I felt considerably less proud of my previous book, *Lettering for Brush and Pen,* principally because I didn't understand the subject at all. It was great fun to write because it was an adventure of sorts, but the end result was, as far as I was concerned, unsatisfactory. That was for Frederick Warne & Co.[175] and I only earned eight pounds from it.

---

175 A British publishing firm famous for the Beatrix Potter series

All in all, I worked for the printing company for four years. That's my record and about all I can stand working for anybody. Or about as long as anyone can stand me. I survived working for Harrap's[176] for two and a half years. During that time I must have done one book cover at least once a fortnight (or every two weeks, in American). So I must have done an enormous number in all. About one hundred and twenty or so, I should imagine.

They were of things like *A History of Fireworks*[177] or *French Made Easy*, or they were sort of documentary books or dark romances. The romances were given to outside artists. They would return great blotchy paintings, the type where at first glance you can't see what anything is, but if you hold it in a particular way it looks like a man with a beard looking out across the horizon. Such effects were well beyond my meager capability. I can only paint in a very clear style, which is often my undoing because if I do it wrong, it's easy for everyone to see that it's wrong.

I didn't keep any of my drawings and paintings. I did keep them for a while when I lived in London because I needed to show them to people to get more work. I sent a lot of them to Harrap's when I applied for the job in their studio. After they saw them they said, "Yes, come and work for us." So they knew in advance that I did book covers. Moreover they knew how long I took and how much I charged for them.

---

176 George G. Harrap & Co. Ltd. nowadays Chambers Harrap Publishers Ltd.
177 By Alan St H. Brock.

Book covers were the only kind of work I did by then. I didn't do any advertisements. Typically I used poster paints which are more of less watercolor paints. They are solid and they have the quality of oil paints but are soluble in water. Back then I think everyone used them. They dry much lighter than they are when wet, which is their difficulty. This meant that if you painted something red, by the time the paint had dried it would end up being pink. You had to take this into consideration when using them.

At the printing company I first worked for a man called Mr. Drake. Then he left. He hated the job and he hated his boss. When he left he said, "I ought to give you some words of advice but I can only say keep on doing what you're doing because it is obvious to me you don't give a damn."

I smiled and nodded.

Then I worked with another man who was a complete fraud and didn't do any work. He went out and sold his own drawings and came back at four o'clock not having been in the office all day. After that, I worked alone before finally I was given my own assistant, which made me feel very grand. I can't remember her name, but she was from Australia and she was very nice. When I eventually left, the foreman said, "Oh, thank God. I was wondering what we were going to do with you."

I left to go to the National Trade Press which was a firm that published trade books. I was only there for about three months because it was so cold I couldn't stay in the office. I don't know why it was freezing. The others didn't seem to mind it. There were five other people working there, but I was the only one who was frozen. I became a freelancer after that. I liked freelancing. When you are freelance, either you can't think how to fill in your time or else you are rushed off your feet.

I don't miss painting. I couldn't paint in the room I'm in now. The light isn't strong enough, my hand is no longer steady and my eyesight is very weak. I suppose I could still do line drawing if I could find my drawing board. It's around somewhere. I'd also need drawing pens, pins and a piece of paper. It would be a bit of an upheaval, really.

I have always written books under the name of Quentin Crisp. I've been Quentin Crisp since I was about twenty-six. I would say the books were written just after the name Quentin Crisp was given to me. I have no regrets about changing my name. It's been very useful. People are saddened though when they learn it isn't my real name which, I suppose, shows that they thought it fitted me adequately.

My real name is Denis Pratt which I was quick to get rid of. It was changed for me by people I knew. I wouldn't have done it otherwise. I haven't got the self-confidence. I've accepted it now and because other people have accepted it, it seems more appealing. When I accepted it in spite of other people, it was difficult to maintain.

My surname was actually given to me by a man called Mr. Palmer who ran a café in Camden Town. He was sympathetic to my cause and the two of us were friends for a time. One night I was sitting with him on his bed eating supper when he asked me to telephone the café he owned. I asked him why and he said it was because he was sure his staff shut up and went home when he wasn't there to watch them.

Since I always do what I am told, I proceeded to telephone the café in question, only to Mr. Palmer's and my surprise someone answered the phone at the other end. They asked me what I wanted. Panic-stricken I turned to Mr. Palmer and said, "What do I want?"

To which he prompted, "Ask if I'm there."

So, I said, "Is Mr. Palmer there?" Obviously he wasn't. He was with me.

"No," they said, "but I will tell him that you called. Who should I say was calling?"

Thinking that I shouldn't give them my real name I turned to Mr. Palmer once more and asked, "Who am I?"

And calmly he said, "You're Mr. Crisp."

I forgot all about the incident, but was reminded about it later in the week. Mr. Palmer had kindly said I could have a meal at his café any time I was passing. So, later that week I ventured to take him up on his offer and made my way to his café. When I arrived and asked, "Is Mr. Palmer here?"

"No, Mr. Crisp," came the reply, "I'm afraid he's not."

And I remembered what had happened and I thought, "Mr. Crisp. That's who I am."

So, for a short while I was Denis Crisp. Until one evening when lots of us sitting around someone said, "You can't go on being called Denis."

I said, "Why not?"

To which they replied, "Oh, it's so feeble."

So I asked, "Well, what should I be called then?"

And people started suggesting a whole host of names in quick succession. When someone suggested 'Quentin' I said, "Stop. That's my name."

It was as if I was holding a divining rod and I had just struck water. And that's how I became Quentin Crisp at the age of twenty-five or twenty-six.

Although everyone came to know me as Quentin Crisp, my name legally remained Denis Pratt for the next fifty-five years or so. Until I came to America.

It was my bank manager, in fact, who said he thought it would be unwise for me to have a passport in one name and use another.

"I think you should legally change your name," he suggested.

So I did. And when I came to pay the lawyer who filled in and filed all the paperwork for me, he wouldn't accept any money. He said: "Just give me a signed copy of your book and that will be enough."

So that's what I did.

So, although I was born Denis Pratt, I will die Quentin Crisp. It's as if it's taken me a whole lifetime to truly find myself, which in a way is exactly what has happened. Even my passport now says Quentin Crisp.

I would never go back to the name Pratt again. That name was a mistake. I don't think my parents had any idea what the word prat means in the wider world. You can make a pratfall in America, which means you fall on your rear end, but things get decidedly worse when you cross the Atlantic. In England, prat is a word describing a certain part of the female anatomy.

I don't think that my mother ever commented on my name as Quentin Crisp. Had she done, I'm sure it would have meant talking about my homosexuality, which we never did. I'm sure she thought there was something illicit about me using a name other than the one I was given at birth. Another possibility was that she was actually quite jealous. She, after all, was a Pratt her entire life and as I have mentioned, she hated the man whose name she took.

CHAPTER 14

The Lower East Side

THE LOWER EAST SIDE OF Manhattan is the home of hopeless cases. You're a hopeless case if, I think, like me, no amount of cajoling and processing can make you join the real world. I could have been taught how to be like a schoolboy but would never have been a schoolboy. The same could be said of my adult life. I'm a hopeless case and nothing could ever be done about it.

I feel at home on the Lower East Side because here, we're all hopeless. Mostly we are unconventional. Sometimes we are foreign. Sometimes we are outcasts. Most of the time we are poor and nearly all of us are outsiders.

There are moves afoot to rename the Lower East Side as 'The East Village'. This will only happen over my dead body. For me, the Lower East Side lacks the 'arty flavor' that makes Greenwich Village so very hard to bear. Greenwich Village is full of girls who nearly got the lead in one of Mr. Shakespeare's[178] plays, and men who are just about to write the

---

178 William Shakespeare, widely regarded as the greatest writer in the English language, 1564-1616

great American novel. On the Lower East Side, nobody has any artistic pretensions. We're the lowest of the low and it's a wonderful place to be. You have the feeling of not being able to get any lower. That's always very nice. From here the only way is up. Things can only get better.

The block that I live on within the Lower East Side is also home to a local chapter of Hell's Angels. They gather and live on the other side of the road to me, nearer to First Avenue. I live nearer to Second Avenue, so I don't ever meet any of them. I only hear them whizzing by on their motorbikes.

Everyone complains that The Hell's Angels keep them awake by driving around with no mufflers on their motorbikes and making a great noise. This, of course, is nonsense. What actually keeps people awake is their indignation. If they lay in bed and thought, "Oh, the Hell's Angels are going by. I wonder where they're going?" They would soon be asleep. Instead they lie in bed, twisting and turning and cursing them through gnashed teeth. "How can they be so selfish? Why do they make all that noise in the middle of the night?" No one would ever get any sleep if they carry on like that.

Nothing attracted me to the Lower East Side. My room was found for me by one of my spies who knew someone who knew someone else who knew the landlord. Thankfully, the landlord consented to let me in. I was in a very difficult position, you see. Most landlords would not let a room to me, but the landlord of my current abode let me one without even seeing me. Perhaps that's why I got it.

I have wandered about the Lower East Side by myself at all hours of the day and night. No harm has ever come to me, much to the surprise, or possibly disappointment, of many of the people who took time out of the busy schedules to warn me of the dangers of living here.

The building I live in is a rooming house. I have one room which is smaller and colder and more expensive than the room in which I lived in London. Otherwise however, it is more or less the same. It's a furnished room so the main things belong to the landlord: the bed, the chair and the washbasin. But the rest is my own. I have remained here because once I had moved in, I was determined never to move again. I shall stay here until I die. In fact, chances are I shall die in this room.

The building I live in is a small building for New York. It is only four floors high. There is a nice flat on the ground floor which has two rooms. It runs from the front of the building to back. I saw it when it was being done up. Of course, such palatial accommodation would never suit me. Two rooms would always be one more than I would need and always one more than I can occupy at any time.

On the next floor, the second floor to Americans, there are two large apartments, each comprising of one room each. I should think they are quite reasonably priced. Above them is the floor on which I live, the third floor, which contains six single occupancy rooms of which mine must be one of the larger ones. The room next to mine is like a cell at the YMCA. Inside there is just enough room for a bed and a smattering of cockroaches. I presume the fourth floor has the same layout as the third, which would mean that, all in all, my building contains fifteen separate lodgings. Typically, tenants in my building are very nice and very quiet.

My room faces the back of the house, which is a disadvantage because the building has no front doorbells. This means I can't sit by the window when I'm waiting for someone whom I've invited to come and see me, to arrive. I'm cut off from the world, but it is wonderful to be in Manhattan and not hear a sound. It's like being in the countryside only without the locals or the boredom.

My room is a sort of L-shaped room. It has a long sort of corridor down one side which leads into the room proper. The livable part of my room is probably about ten feet by twelve feet. It has two windows that face on to the house next door which is so near that the sun never shines into my room. If I want to know what it's like outside, I have to lean out of the window and look up to the sky. The room's walls are a sort of peach color. People have said to me, "Do you like them?"

And I say, "Well, I've never *disliked* them."

I don't tend to think about my surroundings except whether or not a place is convenient to live in or comfortable. My room is very convenient to live in. It has a bed, a chair, a television set, a refrigerator, a bookcase and a hotplate balanced on two milk crates. That's all that I need. Oh, and a washbasin. Contrary to what people might think, I do wash. When people come and look around they say, "Do you have to live here?"

And I say, "Why, shouldn't I?"

They must think I could live in splendor, somewhere. Well, maybe I could for a week or two, but if paid twelve hundred dollars a month for a room, which many people with an apartment do, I would soon be penniless.

I live within my means. I've gotten used to my room and the location of where I live. In this respect I am very much like my sister was. My sister said, "The first thing I do when I move into a new house is set about liking it."

I do the same. At the time of writing I've spent nearly twenty years living here.

My flat in London was larger. It had also had two windows. The main difference is you could walk about my London flat without falling over something, which you can't do here. Oddly, I didn't have a refrigerator or a washbasin in London. I had a bed, of course, and there was a table in the middle of the room and not one but three chests of drawers, so there was a lot more real furniture.

The big difference is that my lodgings in London only cost me six pounds a month. That's about ten dollars or so at the current exchange rate. Here in Manhattan, all this happiness has to be paid for so I am charged three hundred and forty dollars a month for my room, which believe it or not is very cheap for Manhattan, though very expensive compared to England.

I couldn't tell you whether things in general are cheaper or more expensive here because I never really regard the price of anything. As I've said before, I don't really shop. I should say that food costs about the same. Restaurants are cheaper here, especially if someone else pays the bill for you.

I dread spending money, but I can't get away without spending money on rent and the telephone. My telephone is only $14 a month, which again would be a great deal in England, but which is comparably very little here America. People often ask me, "Why don't you have an answering machine?" And the simple answer is, I don't have an answering machine because then I would have to ring people back and that would end up costing me money. I may be a logophile[179] but I don't like the words 'spend', 'buy' or 'purchase'. I prefer words and phrases like 'find', 'come by' and 'happen upon'.

Of course, I've lived alone most of my life. When I first left home I lived with a man, but as I have said before, we were not lovers. I suppose I was born spinsterish. Now of course, I am terribly spinsterish because I've lived alone for so very long. It's what I'm used to. I couldn't bear to live with another person. If anything in my room was moved or wasn't where I'd put it, I would panic. Even though my things are scattered about, I know exactly where everything is.

People have also asked me why haven't I gotten a pet. They must assume that I am lonely, which is far from the truth. They fail to comprehend that I dislike pets intensely and like my own company perfectly well enough without having it interrupted by some slobbering dog or clawing cat. The only advantage of having a pet over a husband or a roommate would

---

179 A lover of words

be that pets don't live as long. But, as I have said already, I am hopeless. I can barely take care of myself. I couldn't possibly be responsible for another living creature. It would be too much.

Living by yourself does tend to mean you lack what others might call 'social graces'. I would never consider myself rude, but I have developed a habit of saying what I mean, though I seldom speak without thinking. If someone mentions war, I don't say, "Oh, that's terrible," out of habit or etiquette or because it's the fashion. If I think something's terrible, I'll say it's terrible and not otherwise. This can sometimes have the odd effect of making people slightly nervous around me, but only, I think, people who are afraid to speak the truth.

People say that brevity is soul of wit, but brevity is in fact the body of wit. The soul of wit is truth. Nothing is funny unless it's also true and we laugh at jokes because we recognize the grains of truth they contain. People think I like to be shocking, but I don't. I merely like to say what I *really* think.

In England, I was accused of talking for talking's sake. When I was so accused, I said, "Would you be angry if I danced for dancing's sake?" To which they merely repeated what they had previously said. What I should have said is, "Would you mind if I lived for living's sake?" That seems to me to be of far greater import whether or not you live your life being true to who you are, which in my case I was.

I don't actually think people believe what I say anyway. Strangers speak to me not to hear the truth, but to hear something funny that they can rush away and repeat to their friends. A sound bite or anecdote, if you will. This I'm used to. I'm not offended by it, except sometimes when I'm being serious and people say, "Oh, you are such a s-s-c-c-ream."

In my head and then out loud, I hear myself saying, "No, I mean it. I was being serious."

And aside from the luxury of time, I have lived without luxury all my life. What I mean by this is that I have lived without material luxury. I was surprised once when someone described me as self-indulgent. When I thought about it, I thought, "Yes. I am self-indulgent when it comes to time. I have plenty of time and I spend it on myself. I don't spend it doing good works. I don't even spend it improving myself or my circumstances." So, in a way they were right.

I wallow in the excess of time that life has given me. A lot of people would say this has been a terrible waste. I would disagree. I don't feel that every hour should be filled with useful occupation. Spare time is the one luxury in which I indulge. Some people never have any time for or to themselves and I am deeply sorry for them. The room in which I spend my time alone however, is devoid of luxury, although this has never bothered me.

When I arrive home from an evening out, I don't come back into my room and sigh at the depravity in which I live. I don't ever remember returning and thinking, "You again. This terrible room." To me, my room is everything I need it to be. I don't need chandeliers or a four-poster bed. I don't need air conditioning or rooms in which to entertain and impress others. I do my entertaining in any number of the rooms provided to the public by New York's bars and restaurants. The world, if you like, is my dining room. This is merely where I rest and sleep.

These days I never open my windows. Since losing the use of my left hand, lifting up the window has become impossible. It's too heavy. Rather than complain however, I have instead come to the opinion that my room is cooler with the windows closed. I think this might even be true.

Even if I could open the windows, the experts on television are advising against it. They want me to stay indoors today because of the risk of low level ozone, whatever that might be. When I was young, ozone was supposed to be good for you. You would go to the seaside and sniff the horrible stink of the sea, and people would say, "It's ozone. It's good for you."

Now it's apparently bad for you. I give up. If there was one thing I would have thought I was safe from here in New York City it's fresh air. I'll just stay here in my room. It's safer and cheaper. And of course, I need to be in just in case the phone rings.

CHAPTER 15

Daily Life

Since I have no curtains in my room to obscure the light, I am woken every morning by sunlight hitting my face. In the summer, I therefore wake at about half past six and in the winter at about half past eight. I rise as soon as I wake up. There is no point in me waiting in bed, hoping that I will feel more awake with just a touch more rest. It doesn't happen.

These days, I don't have breakfast. In fact, I don't typically eat or drink anything until about lunch time. I used to drink a bottle of Guinness for breakfast. I would get out of bed and stagger over to where the Guinness was, open a bottle and drink it. Aside from its alcoholic qualities, Guinness is, of course, a food that you are sustained by. It's like a meal in a bottle. The advantage of drinking it at dawn is also that it shortens the day. With a bottle of Guinness inside, you don't really know that the day has begun until about twelve o'clock, which is nice.

As a rule, around midday I tend to go out to lunch with somebody. This means that my first meal of the day is entirely in the hands of other people. I tend to have whatever people will buy for me. I seldom eat three meals a day. In fact, I usually eat two. Mostly, I like food to be tasteless. For breakfast, which for most people is lunch, I'll have eggs, but I don't care how they come. Scrambled, runny, hardboiled, sunny side up, it's all the same to me. I don't really like bacon very much because here in America bacon is almost all fat. I would say eggs Benedict would be my favorite thing to eat in America. Eggs are nice because they are a minimum risk food and high in protein.

To drink I'll have either orange juice or a sweetened and milky coffee. I'm not big on large meals. A small meal is ample to fortify me until the evening when I'll eat again. Although the texture of food isn't particularly important to me, I'm not a fan of things that are crunchy. I never can understand why advertisements think 'crispy' is a term of praise. When I hear the word it has exactly the opposite effect that the advertisers intended. When I was young I would eat my cereal with warm milk so that I could eat my meal without an awful noise going on about my face.

Despite my English roots, I'm not one for high tea. I very seldom drink tea actually. Typically, I drink tea at home and coffee outdoors. Tea is made so badly in restaurants here that it's really better to drink coffee. So I suppose the fact I rarely drink tea must be because I'm frequently too lazy to make it.

I know lots of people who can't function properly without their morning coffee. They will complain to me about how people "… spoke to me before I had had my coffee." and I say, "How terrible." but really I can't imagine how they feel because I don't feel any different when I drink coffee. When I'm awake, I'm awake and when I'm tired, I go to sleep. I'm very lucky in that regard because, as you know, Ms. Monroe had to be woken with stimulants and put to sleep with sedatives, the poor girl.

From the above you should be able to guess that I am not what could be described as a cook. I rarely cook anything, but this is because I don't really care about what I eat and don't actually like cooking. I can open a tin of soup, fry an egg and boil a potato, but I know these are not skills that will make me a Michelin chef. When it comes to drinking I am much the same. I mostly drink orange juice because that way I don't have to boil a kettle. I'm not a big fan of drinking cocoa or chocolate although if someplace has run out of tea and coffee, they are better than nothing.

I'm a big fan of pudding however. When I was a child, I remember longing for pudding to come. We would have rice pudding, suet pudding, trifle and all other sorts. You can't buy any of those in America, which is a great shame. Over here people confuse pudding with dessert, but they weren't originally synonymous. Traditionally, dessert was a fruit course whereas pudding was a sweet course that followed and consisted of cake or the like. Over the years dessert has come to simply mean that which follows the main course. I suppose the change must have occurred as meals became simplified to typically consist of just three courses.

Crumpets are another misunderstood concept in America. Americans seem to think they are something you would have with tea, which to me makes them sound cake-like. But they typically aren't sweet at all and, in fact, they taste more like a pancake and are best served with butter. You might have them as a snack or for a light lunch. You wouldn't necessarily have them with tea. I'm not sure where America's obsession with crumpets and tea came from. I think Americans' mistake must be in confusing crumpets for scones, but they are altogether different.

America is much more muffin-centric. We used to have muffins when I was little. There used to be a muffin man who walked the streets selling his wares, much in the same way that milkmen and bakers used to sell door-to-door as well. He used to walk through the streets with a tray on his head and a bell which he used to ring. As children we would then rush out into the street, buy half a dozen muffins and then rush back indoors again. I suppose it's similar to the way that children flock to ice-cream vans now.

I like ice cream. I suppose I have a sweet tooth, although I've gotten better as I've gotten older. When I was young, I could eat a whole box of chocolates in the course of an afternoon. I couldn't do it now, but I do still like sweets.

I particularly like American diners and what you might call typical American food: turkey sandwiches, eggs and bacon, corned-beef hash, that sort of thing. I remember when I was young, seeing a film in which someone said, "I don't know if you think I'm always going to be a hash-slinger." I've never seen anyone slinging hash, but I always keep an eye out for it, just in case. The other phrase that baffled me was, "You're nothing but a soda jerk." I mean, how do you jerk soda? Anyway, I don't much like soda, but I do like corned beef hash whether it's slung at me or merely served. I like meals that don't ask very much of me. I don't like meals that challenge me.

In fact, I remember almost dying of starvation in Albuquerque, New Mexico, because I couldn't eat the food. It was too hot. My hosts eventually found something for me to eat, but for some reason they managed to hit upon everything about food that I don't like. I don't like vinegar. I don't like garlic. I don't like anything that would make a meal startling.

When it comes to drink, my favorite tipple is Scotch whisky. I don't like bourbon or Irish whisky though I will occasionally drink the latter. I drink my Scotch without ice because you can't tell what something actually tastes of when it's frozen. I'm no doctor, but I do think Scotch is good for your heart. I think it softens your arteries, making it easier for the blood to flow. This is what I tell myself, anyway.

I was in a restaurant once and had ordered tomato juice without ice. When the waitress brought my drink however, it had ice in it. My host insisted I tell the waitress to take it back and bring back a fresh drink, but this was not necessary. The waitress in question was rushed off of her feet as it was. So, quietly with my coffee spoon, I took the ice out of my drink and placed the cubes one by one into the ashtray. When I had finished I was left with a thimbleful of tomato juice. That's why Americans like you to have ice in your drink.

Despite drinking Guinness in the morning and Scotch on occasion, I should point out that I have never been drunk in the whole of my life. Of course, I've been lightheaded, where my head has been spinning and the whole room has appeared to move around me, but I've never fallen down because I was drunk or not known where I was. I've also never woken up the next morning and not been able to account for my previous night's actions.

In spite of all the above, I enjoy eating out greatly because it gives me the chance to be seen and to interact with an audience. My perfect day would be to be taken out for lunch, to be photographed and recorded and to come back to my flat. Then to go out in the evening again and eat and be photographed and recorded some more.

I never say, "Oh, don't ask me those boring questions." I answer them and smile and try to look as though I've never been asked them before. It's a slight but not a terrible strain. You do have to rally your forces to be around people. It's only afterwards when I am alone in my room recovering, that I rest.

Rereading the above, I sound like the woman at the end of *Uncle Vanya*[180] when the uncle complains of his life and the girl says, "When we are dead, God will be kind to us. We shall smile at our sufferings and we shall rest." When Chekov's plays were originally performed they weren't seen as plays at all. Now when we see them, we realize they're unduly theatrical. That speech is made by a girl who has never mentioned God before but when she sees the curtain coming down, she realizes she's got to say something.

---

180 A play by the Russian playwright Anton Chekhov, 1860-1904

I don't have a daily exercise program or do anything like Ms. Fonda[181] does on her commercials. When I was a model I did exercises. I stood on my head for ten minutes a day because I wanted to get the circulation in my body reversed. But now that I am not a model, I don't do any exercise because I don't want to keep thin. I wouldn't care if I grew to be as fat as a pig, not that it is something that is likely to happen. A lady once asked me, "How do you do it?"

And I told her, "I am consumed perpetually by an inner spiritual flame."

"Oh." She replied, "Well, I think I must be being fed by one."

People also ask me what skin care products I use, but I don't really do anything particularly special. I use Germolene, which is an antiseptic ointment that smells of wintergreen. It can only be obtained in England and it keeps my eczema at bay. But as regards my face, I use Nivea every day in an attempt to keep my skin soft and to protect me from sunburn. I shave every other day, which I find irritates my skin less.

Even at the age of ninety, I still wear makeup. I put it on before I go out anywhere. It's more or less my armor and means I always look the same to people. When I'm wearing makeup, it's as if I'm wearing a mask. People can't tell whether I'm tired or despondent or anything really.

I don't color my hair anymore, but only because one of my hands is paralyzed now and I can't easily manage it. The last

---

181 Jane Fonda, American actress, b. 1937

time I colored my hair, it was violet. I used a coloring I bought from a shop called Manic Panic which used to be on St Mark's Place. The best coloring I ever used were liquids, but the stuff I got from Manic Panic was paste that you mixed with boiling water. When my left hand became paralyzed it became much harder to do the left side of my head. I used to simply brush it on with an old toothbrush, especially at the sides where my hair was the whitest. But you're meant to mix it, put it on, rinse it off and then wait for it to dry. That would have taken two hours though, which I thought was a bit too much.

I never cut my hair now. At the age of ninety I have finally found a way to do my hair. I take some mousse, which looks like shaving foam, and comb it through my hair. Then I put my hat on over the top and only a minimum of hair shows beneath the hat, which I like. I don't like hair though I dislike being bald even more, or half bald as I am. The Dalai Lama[182] might approve of me shaving my head, but I don't think I could live my life as a Buddhist monk. I'm thinking that they would disapprove at my attention seeking and I'm not sure they're allowed to wear makeup or drink Scotch.

Until recently, I never took vitamins. Now I take them. These days I feel positively pickled with tablets. If you were to shake me, I'm convinced I would rattle. I take a tablet of Centrum every day, which is a multivitamin, two aspirins for my heart, an Advil to kill my pain, then there are yellow ones, some blue ones and something else. I'm told I must take the aspirin forever. I believe

---

182 The 14th Dalai Lama, Tenzin Gyatso, b. 1935

they thin the blood and make it easier for my heart to work. Urination is very painful for me at the moment because I have cancer of the prostate gland. It takes a long time as well.

I once told an interviewer that I do nothing on Sundays and she told me, "I don't think you should say that. Couldn't you say that you meditate instead?"

So, I said, "Oh, alright. I meditate."

But actually I do nothing on Sundays. I don't understand why people have a genuine fear of doing nothing and of being alone. Those are the two things that really frighten people. I can't see that it matters. If you are alone, you are alone. You think your thoughts, you putter about, you wash out the crockery and you file your nails.

I never watch television during the daytime because it is so relentlessly jolly. I only ever watch it in the evening. My nightly habit is to peruse the channels and see if there's anything I understand. I flick quickly past anything that looks like baseball, football or basketball. I'll watch the news and almost any drama after about nine o'clock. I like to watch ABC's 20/20. Ms. Walters[183] is a phenomenon to me because her expression never changes no matter how diabolical the question is she's asking you. She turns her round blue eyes towards you and says, "Does it worry you that your lover is fifty years younger than you are?"

She's on Channel 7 which I watch religiously. I used to watch Channel 2, but now I can't really discern the distinction between them.

---

183 Barbara Walters, American broadcast journalist, b. 1929

The news, as I say, is always disastrous. People get run over, people get burned, people fall out of airplanes. I suppose news of disaster elsewhere affirms your own indestructibility. That's the only reason I can think of for its being so popular. You watch as other more mortal men and women succumb to such fates as being run over by a combine harvester or being hit by lightning.

I don't have a favorite television show, but I do have a favorite television show type. I like my programs to be urban, nocturnal and threatening. So my favorite show is, I think, either *The Practice* or *NYPD Blue*. I watch them every week, but I understand that they are coming to an end. *Law and Order* is pretty good as well, but I like *The Practice* and *NYPD Blue* the best.

I like those two programs because the good guys don't always win. Mr. Mason,[184] who was wonderful, always won. He only ever seemed to have to work out who had done it and how. He would always be right. But in *The Practice* they don't always win, which to me makes it much more realistic. I mean, look at some of the verdicts coming out of America's court system these days.

When I'm at home alone, I don't wear shoes. I potter around barefoot. It takes me about two and a half hours to get myself ready to go out these days. If I'm staying in however, I just wrap myself up in my dressing gown and stay undressed. I don't sleep in pajamas unless I'm away from home. In hotels

184 Perry Mason, fictional defense attorney created by Erle Stanley Gardner, 1889-1970

I wear pajamas in case a member of the staff rushes into the room in the middle the night for some emergency or other.

Recently, I've begun to have dreams again. This has surprised me because for many years I would sleep soundly and dreamlessly. I had a dream last night. The whole thing was a sort of yellowish-greenish color, and I remember thinking, "Why is this color in the room?" I was in a wonderful room with a soft light as though it were summer and I were in a garden, outdoors. I was there with a lot of other people. When I got into the room, I started to play chess in my head with someone standing nearby. Now, I can only play chess in very perfunctory way, so as soon as I realized I was playing a game in my head, I knew I was dreaming and woke up. It was about seven o'clock in the morning.

When I was a child I had the most fearful dreams. I dreamed that people were pursuing me. They came down the streets, moving as though on wheels. I would throw myself on the pavement and cover myself with a cloth in order not to been seen. Then I would look up through a hole in the cloth and see them all looking at me. Someone who analyzes dreams told me my dream reflected a desire by me not to be perceived, which I thought was rather obvious. Of course, the opposite is true of me now I am in the profession of being.

Not long ago I dreamed I was still a model, and I went to a large art school and took off my clothes and laid on a throne. The students came into the room, but instead of painting me, went over to a far window and started to work on some other project that didn't concern me at all. This made me anxious.

Was I supposed to be here? So I put on a shirt and went into the next room only to find another class who were all standing around waiting for a model to arrive. This upset me greatly as no model wants to keep a class waiting, nor does any human being want to look like a fool. When I woke up, I continued to be upset. It's interesting how dreams can alter your mood in real life.

I once knew a woman who claimed that she had never slept. She did, of course, but what she meant was that she woke up so early that it made her worry that she would not feel alert and well when the day finally came. I said to her, "Can't you just lie there with your eyes shut and think about nothing?"

And she said, "No. Of course I can't."

What kept her awake, once she had awoken, was the anxiety that she would not sleep again.

I'm certain that when we die, we do not dream. I was once asked what I would wear to a party to celebrate the end of the world. It's an odd notion since it would mean curtains for everyone. I welcome death, but I know many people who aren't as keen to make death's acquaintance. My answer however, was that I would wear more or less whatever I've got. I never buy anything special to wear for any event. I've only got four shirts: one of them pink, one of them blue, one of them mauve and one of them green. When the end of the world comes I shall be wearing one of them. Also, I only have two suits: one of them blue and one of them gray. I shall be wearing one of them as well, when the end of the world comes.

Of course, if I am too ill and happen to be in bed for the big event, I shall be wearing a dressing gown. So, I wouldn't dress up for the party at the end of the world, but I would at least dress.

CHAPTER 16

On Being Ninety

As I WRITE THESE WORDS, I am ninety years old. My nineti-eth birthday passed last year on December 25th 1998.

The only advantage of being ninety, as opposed to being sixty, seventy or eighty, is that one can look forward to death with greater certainty. When you're sixty or seventy, the thought of death crosses your mind like a shadow. It disturbs you and worries you. By the time you reach my age you are longing for it.

Yes, the world around me may be getting noisier, sexier and more horrible by the minute, but at least I can comfort myself with the fact that the end is in sight. Or so I thought. Imagine my horror when I opened the newspaper just the other day and discovered they will soon be able to make us all live until we turn one hundred and thirty. It doesn't bear thinking about.

The truth is my body is dying on me. These days I carry it around like a horrible old overcoat. As you get older and older, your body begins to decay. You start to smell of death and there's nothing you can do about it.

My eyesight has deteriorated to the point where I can no longer see properly. I should wear glasses when I go out, but I am far too vain for facial clutter. As a result, when I venture outside I walk the streets nearly blind.

To add to this, I am also now partially deaf. This means I appear to ignore the greetings of friends and mishear the inquiries of strangers. The deafness combined with my blindness results in people talking to me as if I'm a non-comprehending child, which can be annoying if not used to one's advantage. Nevertheless, I remain perfectly capable of comprehending what someone might say to me, were I actually able to see the person in question and hear the words they speak.

It doesn't really matter since my legs have given up on me as well. These days I spend more time working out how to avoid making the trip downstairs from my apartment than I ever spend outdoors. When I do get out, I can barely walk more than a few yards and only manage that at a snail's pace.

According to those who know, I'm apparently very lucky. Supposedly I'm in good shape for my age. This can only mean there are some very unfortunate aged souls out there in even worse shape than me.

The dream of living longer, of living forever, is a young person's dream. Writers have often dreamed of immortality. Mr. Swift[185] in *Gulliver's Travels*[186] told us about the Struldbrugs who devised a way of living long past their sell-by date. What a pathetic sight they were. Then, of course, there was Mr. Shaw

---

185 Jonathan Swift, Anglo-Irish writer, 1667-1745
186 First published in 1726

and his tragic *Methuselah* [187]. If memory serves me right, and naturally that is one of the first things to go, he lived for a thousand years. What a curse that proved.

No, ours isn't a world for old people. Every few minutes there are adverts on the television telling you how to keep young and how to keep lines from appearing on your face. But when you're ninety you don't just have lines on your face, you have them all over your entire body. Everything today is geared towards the young, which leaves a terrible feeling of exclusion within even moderately old people.

Where would we all hide if we lived to be one hundred and thirty? Think of the gadgets we'd need. Every house would need its own elevator. "Ah, but the world would be so much wiser," say the optimists. I can't see it myself because as we get very old we lose our wisdom, our language and eventually our mind. If we all lived forever we'd end up with a world in which no one could communicate. We'd all have forgotten how to.

For me, the absolute nothingness of death is a blessing. Something to look forward to. If I discovered a potion that enabled people to live until they were one hundred and thirty, the first thing I would do is bury it.

When asked whether it is better to be young and healthy or old and wise, I would say it depends. You can be both in the course of a lifetime, but I wouldn't put one higher than the other. More important, I think, is that that people act their

---

187 *Back To Methuselah* by George Bernard Shaw, published 1921

age. I would like to think I always have. I've never sought to be young, to be more innocent than I am or to know more than I do. But as I said before, the memory is one of the first things to go.

Though I would never describe myself as old and wise, the closest I came to that particular combination was when I turned seventy and came to America for the first time at the invitation of Mr. Bennett.[188] I returned to America two years later to live and it was the best decision I ever made. At the age of seventy I was adventurous. Now I am ninety I am a stick in the mud.

I celebrated my seventieth birthday in England, probably with a minimum of fuss. It just came and went. People made a great deal of fuss for my ninetieth birthday, however. I was performing at the Intar Theatre on 42nd Street on my actual birthday which like every other of my birthdays, occurred on Christmas Day. The trouble with being born on Christmas Day is you're never quite sure whether the air of celebration that exists is for you or You-Know-Who. It makes no difference, really.

Anyway, a letter of congratulations arrived for me and was pinned up on the wall of the theatre's foyer. It was from Mr. Clinton.[189] From the White House. Well, everybody looked at it very carefully and fingered it. They couldn't decide whether it was a fake or if it was real. It turned out

---

188 See footnote #145

189 President William Jefferson Clinton, 42nd President of the United States from 1993 to 2001, b. 1946

to be genuine and I think it's wonderful that Mr. Clinton should care enough about me, an alien, an outsider, to write to me on my birthday.

People say the letter demonstrates the importance of who I am and what I've meant to people throughout the world. I suppose it's because of my fame, or rather my infamy since I am famous for no good reason. Whatever it is, I enjoy it because, as far as I know, the only reward of fame is that it extends your social horizon and it remains my ambition to meet everyone in the world before I die.

Nothing about turning ninety has astonished me. Only the fact that it is of such interest to other people. I regard turning ninety as an affliction, but the American public regards it as an achievement. This I find very strange because you don't achieve it, it just happens to you. I've gotten used to it now. If people say, "We hear you're ninety,"

I smile and say, "Yes, isn't it terrible?"

These days, of course, I ignore my birthday. When I was young, you have birthday presents, and cards, and things like that and you celebrate it as if you're marching forward on some great quest and you have just reached another milestone. Had my ninetieth birthday not coincided with the opening night of my one-man show, I would not have taken any notice of it. It's not that I'm not keen on reaching my destination, I have said as much to the contrary, it's that these days I don't have the energy. Plus, not making a big deal about my own birthday means I don't have to feel guilty when I fail to remember other people's.

Birthday presents become less important as you get older, as well. When you're young you can write lists of all the spoils and trinkets your heart desires. These days I can't think of anything that I long to have. So, I accept whatever I am given. I don't like joke presents. I don't like to open envelopes which are full of confetti or glitter and which spill all over the room when you open them. Other than that though I receive gifts gladly and I try to remember to write to the people who give them and thank them.

When my life is over, I would like to think people could say of me, "He kept his word." I never put off or dismiss things and think, "Oh, well, they can lump it. I can't be bothered with that." It's not that I have any particular morality, I just deal with people as cozily as I can. A woman once wrote to me and sent me a copy of *The Naked Civil Servant* and said, "Will you sign this for my son's birthday? His name is William. He came out to me and I am trying to support him as much as possible." Well, I ended up losing her address and it made me unconscionably sad.

I can't imagine what's been the best gift I've ever received. I received a walking stick for my ninetieth birthday and various scarves. I also received a package of food, which was very nice. The overcoat I'm wearing now was a gift. It's wonderfully light. I can't wear heavy clothes these days because it makes it so hard for me to walk. A man once gave me a pair of shoes and I remember wearing them for years. I'd hoped I would die before they wore out. Sadly they wore out before I did.

I suppose I'm just not good at celebrating things. I don't want to wear a funny hat or jump about in streams. I don't want to shout and sing. I probably don't celebrate holidays because my life has been one big holiday. As I once said of Halloween, "Oh, I shan't be bothered. I'll not get dressed up in fancy clothes."

To which my friend replied, "You're always in fancy clothes."

And that, of course, is true. I wear what I want all the time, so I don't have any need to dress up for anything.

The fact that I have turned ninety astonishes me. When I was young I never expected to live as long as this. Neither did anyone else. A spring never came without someone saying, "We never thought you'd live through another winter." I never thought I appeared as frail as that to other people, but evidently I did. I was very frail when young, and I liked being frail. When I was born I had pneumonia. I was always sick. I suppose I got tougher as time went by.

When I went out into the world, I was never ill. I don't think I was ever absent from a job due to sickness my whole life. Except when my wisdom tooth impacted. I went to a dentist, swooned and said dramatically, "What will become of me?" And he simply took out the tooth next to it on which it was pressing and the pain passed.

At ninety, I do feel less well than I used to feel. I feel inadequate to cope with things, unable to walk to places because they are too far. You don't need advice on growing old, because it overtakes you. It's irresistible. You have to accept your fate which is to be overlooked and, to some extent, to be ridiculed.

You become a victim as you get older, a victim of young people. Mostly they overlook you, which can sometimes be nice because then you don't have to bother. But if they say you are old fashioned, you have to accept it and say "Yes, I am old fashioned." If Boy George says I'm old-fashioned, then I am. It doesn't worry me. I don't try to answer it or try to improve myself so that I become 'new-fashioned'. It's not necessary.

Now I'm old, I've accepted my limitations. I don't want to be president. I don't want to rule anything in particular. I live in a house which belongs to somebody else, and I have no desire to own my own home. It would be a burden I would have to think about all day.

In fact, I've never really owned anything. The furniture in my room isn't mine. Almost nothing around me is. A few things are, like cups and saucers and things like that, but my general lack of possessions makes me happy since I don't feel weighed down by them. I don't mean to say I'm not materialistic, people who profess as much tend to suggest they are some kind of spiritual being above earthly things. That is certainly not a description that fits me. I like comfort, but I like perfectly ordinary things. I eat, I drink, I sleep and don't really care how much I earn so long as it's enough to live on.

Now I'm ninety, I am constantly feeling tired. My body is a continuing nuisance. When I was young, if I wanted to reach for something I'd stretch out my arm and grab it. Now I'll think it's too far, I can't be bothered and that I'll simply do without instead. Walking across my small room has become such an effort that I am increasingly leaving things undone. It used to take me twenty minutes to walk to the post office on 11th Street. Now it would take me forever and I'd have to stand when I got there, so I try not to go.

Today I feel better than I have in a long time, but that's because I recently cancelled all my engagements. You wouldn't think that lunching and talking with people could be so tiring. You don't notice it at the time. You don't come back feeling utterly exhausted, but somehow it catches up with you and in the end you long to just lie down and be silent.

Being ninety means you have to plan your day to cause as little strain as possible. I try not to go up and down stairs more than twice a day. Yesterday I went to pay my income tax, came back and got my shirts from the cleaners and carried them back to my apartment all in one go. Ms. Davis[190] said, "Old age is not for sissies." and she was right.

These days my memory is very bad, which is sad because it adds a note of condescension to my relations with people. People ring me up and say, "This is John, don't you remember me?"

And I say, "I'm working on it."

Then they'll try and jog my memory. "I come from Pittsburgh, don't you remember?"

And they will keep that up and add bits of what they have said before, but, of course, I still can't remember them. In the

---

190 Bette Davis, American actress, 1908-1989

end I'll say, "It doesn't matter whether I remember you or not. I am pleased to hear whatever you have to say."

But that's not enough for them, they want to be remembered.

I'm beginning to think I was born with Alzheimer's disease because nowadays I can't remember anybody. Then, the other day someone told me that people with advanced Alzheimer's disease can't even remember who they are, which is terrifying. They say that Ronald Reagan[191] doesn't know who he is. It's so difficult to imagine because all anyone's really got is who they are.

Although I'm relatively free of pain from the prostate cancer I've been diagnosed as having, the discomfort of my eczema is a living hell. My shoulder and the backs of my hands are particularly bad. I want to scratch myself until my skin is raw, but that would do more harm than good. It burns. I wish I could stop it, but I don't know how.

I am told never to wash because as I dry myself I will inadvertently remove the outer layer of my skin. So I only wash the bits that matter, under my arms and things like that. I never wash my ankles or my feet because it irritates them. I've tried every kind of cream and ointment imaginable, but nothing brings me relief.

Some say I am the world's oldest living homosexual, but of course no one can be sure. The fact that my turning ninety caused such a stir in New York society must mean there aren't many people like me that have done such a thing. The past

---

191 Ronald Reagan, 40th President of the United States from 1981 to 1989, 1911-2004

year has been a crazy one for me. I still do the same work; I still live in the same way, but turning ninety has sort of worked everyone up.

Should I reach one hundred, I hope to be in bed propped up with pillows, preferably alone and waiting for death with open arms. I knew a woman in England who wrote to her mother and said, "Don't resist death."

Her mother wrote back and said, "I'm not resisting it. When it comes I shall say, 'What kept you?'"

I have no plans to move, so I imagine I will die in my apartment. Until then I shall be here in this room waiting for death. Mr. Williams[192] said he went home and waited for death, and someone was very annoyed about that, but I understood perfectly what he meant. That's what you're doing really. Unless you have some greater purpose, some goal to which you're working your way. I'm not doing any of that. I'm just filling in time pleasantly.

I would hate to live to be a hundred because I feel pretty inadequate now. If I can't remember what happened yesterday or can't walk at all then life will be a mess. With luck, I will die within the next two years and that will be a great relief, not only to me, but to many.

I've been asked many times if I believe in God, which I take to mean, do I believe in a god. In one theater where I said, "I will answer this question, but would not like to cause anyone any offence," a man in the audience interjected with,

---

192 Kenneth Williams, English comedian and writer, 1926-1988

"Why stop now?" Of course, I like to tease, but it's never my intention to offend.

My feeling is we invented God, not that God invented us. I think that man invented God so as to have some reason to account for the idea of absolutes. We know what virtue is, we know what sin is, we know what bravery is and we know what cowardice is only if we invent God to sit in the middle and judge all of these notions. Otherwise, they don't have any meaning.

I can believe in a god if God is the thing that encloses the universe, the thing that causes things to happen, but I cannot believe in a god susceptible to prayer. These days I never pray and when I did as a child it was nothing more than drama practice.

Mr. Tennyson[193] said he couldn't live if prayer went unregarded, which is an extraordinary thing to have said. He must have believed in God. I believe he was an educated man, but I suppose he must also have been superstitious. Why did he believe that if you prayed you altered your fate? It seemed to me so unlikely. It seems to me too humiliating to bargain with The Almighty. Why should he give you a bicycle with ten speeds simply because you didn't eat sweets during Lent? It makes no sense.

Religion has no place in my life. Blind faith is, I think, a belief in God in spite of everything. Every argument to the contrary is cast aside. People want to believe in God and they

---

193 See footnote #3

want to believe in him absolutely. Contradiction they wave aside. They don't bother to investigate more rational explanations for why life is the way it is. I suppose people that want to believe in God so badly are insecure in themselves.

There is a theory that if we didn't believe in God we would all behave appallingly. I don't find that to be so. I don't find that atheists behave any worse than anybody else. I think you have to behave nicely for the sake of other people, not for the sake of some spirit who is watching you from above and judging you. It seems to me, you judge yourself and other people judge you and you have to live by their standards and by your own. Not by some absolute standard which no one can live up to.

I'm always surprised that God is 'so angry'. It seems to me that if you have absolute power, you can afford to behave nicely. But the god of the Muslims promises you a seat in paradise if you murder a Christian. Christianity is nearly as bad. The Christian god allegedly said, "I am a jealous god. Thou shalt have no other gods before me." Now, why would he say that? If I were God, and I never can make out why I am not, I would say, "Well, shop around. If you find anything that fits you better, stick with it." Then I would wink and say, "But I'll be seeing you." I wouldn't prevent people from believing in other gods. I would just assume they'll eventually realize they've made a mistake and come back to me and in the meantime I would busy myself with more important things.

There's a poem which says, "O Sons of Men, when all is flame, what of your fame and splendor then? When all is fire and flaming air, what of your rare and high desire to turn the clod to a thing divine, the earth a shrine, and man the God?" The meaning is, of course, that nobody's reputation lives forever. Even the names of Alexander The Great[194] and Genghis Khan[195] will disappear when the world ends. I don't think anything is immortal, certainly not a god.

It doesn't worry me. If God exists I don't think he's angry with me. I have recently learned that Mother Teresa said we should treat all people as though they were at least better than ourselves and that strikes me as a wonderful thing to have said. It alters your whole way of living. I wouldn't act in such a way because God is watching me however, I would do it because it seems a satisfactory way of going on.

Should there be a heaven inhabited by some god, I hope that if I arrived there he or she would say, "Welcome." I would find it rather disconcerting to be greeted with, "Watch your step." I wouldn't want to be in a heaven in which you are in constant danger of being chucked out.

Because I don't believe in God, I therefore do not believe in the devil. To my mind evil simply resides in people who wish to harm other people. I think it's as simple as that. If no one wished harm to anyone, if they wished always to spare them harm then the world would be an easier place to live in.

In spite of my cancer, I only started thinking seriously about death last year when my heart became bad. I would gladly go now, but I'm a sissy and I can't throw myself out of

---

194 Alexander III of Macedon, 356 BC-323 BC
195 Genghis Khan, Great Khan and founder of the Mongol Empire, c. 1162- 1227

a window or in front of a train or something drastic like that. I had thought about throwing myself at a policeman, but even that's been done now and were I to do likewise I would just be accused of plagiarism. The man in question bought a toy gun, according to the newspaper, pointed at the police and they shot him.[196] They later found a letter in his pocket thanking them. I thought that was wonderful. His was what I would call a significant death.

---

196 Probably 19-year old Moshe Pergament of Manhasset Hills, shot November 14, 1997

CHAPTER 17

My Significant Death

A SIGNIFICANT DEATH IS A death which somehow gets into everybody's mind so that nobody says, "Isn't he dead? I thought he was dead." You want to die in such a way that everyone knows and remembers your death. This means you have to die by yourself.

You don't want to die on the same day somebody of significance dies. Princess Diana[197] died at the same moment that Mother Teresa[198] died, and somehow it all got muddled up and they both became saints at the same moment. Had Diana died on a different day there might have been a more sensible assessment of her character.

I don't mind what season I die in or what place. People don't seem to like it when people die alone. I remember once praising Ms. Crawford[199] and someone in the audience said, "You praise her, but she died alone and an alcoholic." What's

---

197 Diana, Princess of Wales, first wife of Charles, Prince of Wales, 1961-1997

198 The Blessed Teresa of Calcutta, Albanian-Indian Roman Catholic nun and missionary,1910-1997

199 Joan Crawford, American actress, 1904-1977

wrong with dying alone? If you die in the presence of other people you have to be polite and die. That seems to me to add insult to injury.

I would like to die alone in my room. Somebody died in one of the other rooms of my building and they were found the very next day. I don't know what caused anyone to look in their room and find them lying on the floor, but something did. I suppose if I didn't answer the telephone people would eventually come knocking at my door and when I didn't open it they might conclude that I was dead.

The other day I received a letter saying I was a fraud. That I longed for death but kept on living. I can see their point. It's not that I'm a fraud however, it's that I'm not capable of the suicide that would bring my life to a close. I couldn't inflict violence upon myself or pain.

I used to know a lady who hanged herself. That must take hours to die. You tie something around neck and then you hang it on a hook and you jump off a chair. But you don't die for hours. It can't be a pleasant way to go and yet that's what she did. She was about forty, I suppose. I never dreamed she would do such a thing. I knew she was unhappy, but I didn't know she was as desperate as that. Her suicide occurred over twenty years ago when I was living in England.

I had hoped Mr. Clinton would declare a limit on the number of days we are allowed to live, but he didn't. It seems perfectly reasonable to me that, at the age of say, seventy-five, you would receive a telegram from the White House saying, "We congratulate you on reaching your seventy-fifth birthday and hope to see you in the Forgetting Chamber at 4:30 p.m." Then an unmarked van would arrive, you would get into it and be taken to the town hall and put to sleep the way animals are.

Such certainty would enable *planning*. You would make arrangements regarding your possessions and money and would not have to leave anything to chance. As it is, you cling on to everything because you feel you will go on living indefinitely. I feel I've lived too long. I repeat myself incessantly and I take up time and space. One of the hate letters I received said I was a waste of space, and I am.

When I came to America, I found that everybody was my friend and friendship is certainly a good substitute for love. As the end of my life approaches I can't say that I have been loved because I don't really know what love means. Instead I can say I am content with my relations with other people. When people say they love me, I can only say thank you. I do not say, "I love you," back.

I found three hate letters the other day. They all end with 'Drop dead.' and 'Go to Hell.' and other expressions like that. I don't know why people are so angry with me. In England the gay community accepted me, while heterosexuals did not. Here the heterosexuals accept me, while the gay people do not. I can't help it. I can't calculate what the gay community wants.

I was never more surprised than how angry Ms. Clausen[200] was when I said that a pregnant woman should have the right

---

200 See footnote #47

to abort her fetus if she knew it was gay. She was very upset. She said I've made it easier for people to beat up homosexuals. Obviously, I didn't want them murdered, I wanted them never to be born, which is different. Very different. What I was proposing was an act of compassion. I wouldn't wish what I have suffered throughout my life on anyone.

Ms. Clausen kept referring to the fact that people had more social persecution in my day than they have now. She may be right. Of equal concern to me though are the horrors of homosexual life: the cavorting in men's lavatories and darkened rooms in public houses. That too might have changed without my knowing, but it is the degradation homosexuals suffer that I am so keen they avoid. When it comes to sex, I am happy now, because I haven't bothered with sex for more than fifty years.

I don't believe in life after death. The idea of once more falling out of your mother's womb with the words, "Here again." is too much for me to bear. I never understand why Ms. MacLaine[201] espouses the notion of reincarnation. This life alone has left me weary enough that I would gladly forgo all my future lives. I hope that death is just nothing.

If we do reincarnate after this life, I want to come back as a woman. I feel I am suited to the life of a woman and have not been suited to the life of a man as I have said earlier in this book. That has been my trouble. I wouldn't mind what sort of woman I came back as, the same class and the

---

201 Shirley MacLaine, Oscar-winning American actress, b. 1934

same nationality as I have now would do. I wouldn't want to have a grand life. I wouldn't want to find that I was a duchess or something. I wouldn't want to be beautiful because I wouldn't want to be sought after or anything weird like that, but I wouldn't want to be hideous either. Preferably I would have a job that's not too taxing which I could do satisfactorily while waiting for life to pass.

I don't like the countryside now, but I might like it more if I were a woman and could live there in some kind of comfort. I don't like nature, I like people, chiefly women. In this life I would like to have been a middle-class woman surrounded by more or less the same and to have played bridge well enough for people not to dread having me as a partner.

I don't like nature because it's so lonely and does nothing for you. People say that it's wonderful to look at, but I never look at anything, so I don't really long to stare at the clouds or the sky or the trees or the grass or anything like that. I'm not interested in what things look like. I don't see any spirituality in nature.

People are always trying to sell it to me. We have conversations which begin, "Well it's nice to get out of city at times, isn't it?"

And I say, "No."

"Very well, to get fresh air into your lungs, then?"

And I say, "No."

I would like the whole of North America to be paved over and, if possible, to have a glass roof put over the whole thing, like a huge Grand Central Station.

When I was younger, I think I probably thought of myself as poetic rather than spiritual, someone uninterested in this world or in making money. I don't think that's the same as being spiritual though. Being useless isn't the same as being spiritual and I've been useless all of my life.

When you're useless, you have to be able to appeal to people to help you, which I learned to do. Being useless is not the same as being hopeless, but people use the words interchangeably. "Oh you are hopeless." They say it, snatch whatever it is away from you and make it work. But they don't really mean you are without hope. They mean *they* are without hope for you. I did have hope in a time gone by, but now I don't have any hope at all.

I don't believe I have a soul. I would say the soul is a human invention inspired by fear. It protects people from the notion that they die when their body dies. When my body dies, I don't visualize that my soul will take wing and fly out of the window toward the sky. I think I will stay here and I shall be dead.

Can one die stylishly? I think you can. You must die without trying to get the world's pity. You mustn't let any guilt fall on anybody. So, if you commit suicide, you must explain why you've done it so that nobody feels they should have stepped in or seen it coming. People are always saying, "I should have known, I should have seen the signs." This is rubbish. People who commit suicide don't want anyone to see the signs.

Anyway, you can't win. If you fail to commit suicide people say, "Well it's just a call for attention," but it isn't. Typically those who try unsuccessfully succeed in doing so at a later date. I remember there was an actress, I forget her name, who tried to kill herself and her husband found her at it and prevented it from happening. She tried again, successfully, twenty-five years later, so she was always thinking, "I can still do it."

I would never kill myself, but I've thought about it. I was in touch with the Hemlock Society which sent me a book telling me everything I needed to know. It was so elaborate. I had to go to Mexico in order to buy a specific drug, then I had to get it past customs on the way back and drink it at once along with something, having taken my shoes off or something. I have never attempted suicide, so I don't or can't say how far I would go. When I hear of people who have however, I am filled with admiration that they managed to get away with it.

Suicide seems perfectly sensible to me, if one wants to avoid being a nuisance to those surrounding us. Otherwise our friends and family feel obliged to help us throughout terminal illnesses, saying things like, "You look better today," and the other lies that accompany bunches of flowers and boxes of chocolates. You know you don't look better and you want to die.

I don't think it's right to kill yourself to get out of a mess you yourself have created though. To my mind you can't commit suicide so as not to pay your debts. I think you're obliged to tidy everything up first before you pop your clogs. I've tidied up everything as far as I can. This has involved throwing away everything that's useless in my apartment with the exception of me.

I think doctor-assisted suicide is perfectly acceptable. I don't know why people are so cross with Dr. Kevorkian.[202] He only kills people who long for death. Why should they be made to stay alive? Just because the idea of killing them is connected with the idea of murder? This is a nonsense spread by the same fundamentalists that equate masturbation with infanticide.

Of concern to me is whether or not I have a heart attack, something all too likely from what my doctors are telling me. I don't know what that would be like, but my biggest fear is dying temporarily only to be brought back by some method of resuscitation. I would rather they leave me lying dead on the floor. I would not know any different, so a heart attack would do quite nicely. That would be dying in style.

Once dead, I want to be cremated because I don't really want a funeral service. I don't want anyone to have to stand in the pouring rain in a churchyard around an empty hole, while someone explains how wonderful I was. That would be respectively miserable, morbid and untrue. I've gone and that's that. I don't mind the idea of a memorial service though because that might be jolly. Then everyone who ever knew me can meet in some place and talk about how awful I was.

I don't want my ashes spread over the sea or any of that rubbish. Just get rid of them. Throw them in the Hudson River if you want.

---

202 Jacob Kevorkian, American pathologist and euthanasia activist, 1928-2011

When people ask me how I want to be remembered, I think they imagine themselves leaning down from a cloud and counting the people at their funeral. A woman once said to me, "You don't *know* that there's nothing afterwards."

To which I replied, "I don't *know* that tomorrow will come, but it does."

I see nothing around me that lives that after it dies. Why should we live? Who are we that we are so special or important? I assume that death is death and I'm very glad it is because one of the nicest things you can say about life is that it will end.

I don't care how I am remembered. If you suppose I will look down from a cloud and find that I have been misunderstood or misquoted, you are wrong. I would be annoyed but I shall be dead, so what does it matter?

I am told Mr. Shaw[203] has left instructions that his epitaph reads: "Go away." That's nice. On my tombstone, not that there will be one, I suppose it could say my name, but who wants to know that I'm lying there? It seems to me that epitaphs and tombstones exist only for those who weep for the dead and bring them flowers. In which case, the perfect epitaph for me would be "I am not worthy."

Yes, that would be lovely.

---

203 Artie Shaw, American composer and actor, 1910-2004

QUENTIN ONCE SAID THAT AN autobiography is an obituary in serial form with the last chapter missing. In his case, because we finished the content for this third installment of his autobiography four months before he passed away in July 1999, there is not much missing. Even so, this afterword will fill in what little of Quentin's story remains untold by him. This is his missing last chapter.

I first encountered Quentin when I was around 18 years old and saw the movie version of *The Naked Civil Servant* by accident on Kentucky Educational Television. I believe it was 1976. Only a few years earlier in 1973, the American Psychiatric Association removed homosexuality from its Diagnostic and Statistical Manual of Mental Disorders. Back then growing up gay in Eastern Kentucky, especially in the kind of fundamentalist Christian environment that I was raised in, meant living in fear. Fear of ostracism, fear for your liberty, and with the KKK a very real threat, fear for your life.

We had been watching television as a family, and my mother had been flicking through the channels to find something suitable for us all to watch. Quite how we ended up watching *The Naked Civil Servant*, I have no idea, but watch it we did. The rest of my family scoffed and jeered throughout the broadcast. I, on the other hand, having known I was gay since the age of seven or eight, was transfixed. Seeing Quentin in my living room, a resilient, self-assured and openly gay man, gave me more courage and strength than I can convey. It didn't matter that he was fifty years older than me, it didn't matter that he was describing life in another country, and it didn't matter that I couldn't relate to his flamboyant, some would say feminine, appearance. He spoke to me directly and gave me the thing that Harvey Milk would later insist every gay man needed: hope. He told me it was okay to be who I was, though I knew I could never be that person in Eastern Kentucky.

I moved to New York on Friday, July 13, 1979. It's an easy date to remember. I'd finished college and wanted to begin my adult life in the same surroundings as the poet Edna St. Vincent Millay. That meant moving to Greenwich Village and in 1983 that is what happened when I moved in with my lover, Charles Barron. Charles lived on Christopher Street only four blocks away from Millay's townhouse, and that is where I built my life for the next 26 years. Quentin moved to New York in 1981 and, though I saw him perform a number of times in those early years, it was not until February 1986 that I finally got to meet him.

I was working as an editor for a company called Business Research Publications when my secretary, Kathy Hurt, came back from lunch one day unusually excited. She told me she had just met Quentin Crisp while in the line for stamps at the East Village post office. After confirming that she *had* actually met Quentin (a brief description was sufficient since who else in the world looked or dressed like Quentin?), Kathy lamented that she hadn't formally introduced herself to him. Not a problem, I told her. He's in the phone book! She should call him up and arrange to have dinner with him and, that way, I could come along and meet him as well (I confess that until then I had always lacked the confidence to reach out directly to Quentin myself).

So that is how, aged 29, I first came to meet Quentin over dinner at Las Ventanas on the corner of Christopher Street and Bleecker Street. In hindsight, a Mexican restaurant was a terrible choice for a dinner date with Quentin since he hated spicy food. At the time though, I had no idea. Quentin famously never said 'no' to anything, especially a free meal. Without question, he was wined and dined by many thousands of people over the course of his lifetime. So exactly what turned our initial meeting into a relationship that lasted the next thirteen years, I couldn't tell you. Quentin actively avoided second rendezvous dates because he typically used up all of his best one-liners and anecdotes on the first.

Why or how then did Quentin and I become friends? Well, there was certainly a spark or a bond between us as early as that first encounter. Not a romantic spark you understand, though in subsequent years rumors persisted that he and I were having some kind of affair. That amused us both. I can say however, that having observed a number of people over the years around Quentin, by comparison to them I neither asked for nor demanded anything from him. Unlike others, I did not try to use Quentin to embellish myself.

My relationship with Quentin was similar to that between a father or a mother and their son, especially so since my own father had died when I was eleven or twelve. The age gap between us certainly supported our respective roles in that scenario, but the warmth I had for Quentin came not from a blood relationship, but from a desire to help him in any way that I could. It was true love. Distilled further, I wanted to make sure that everything he had given to me and the rest of the world was repaid back to him. One positive aspect of my restrictive Christian upbringing was that at least I had been raised to give back.

Over the next few years, I saw Quentin every week. Then at least twice a week. Then even more frequently. He inhabited a different world from me, his professional or celebrity world which I never knew or tried to be a part of. Instead, I knew Quentin as a private person. The real Quentin was different from his public persona, but just as fun and entertaining. Quentin never criticized others in public, nor did he curse, but in private it was altogether a different matter. We cooked for one another (Charles and I more so than he), we would take him to dinner at his favorite restaurant – the now-defunct Sazerac House – and we shared birthdays, Christmases and other celebrations together.

As he became frailer, I began to help him not just with errands and chores but also with his work. When he lost the use of his left arm, I helped him continue writing by taking his dictation and typing up his essays and articles. My role in his life eventually merged that of friend, family member, personal assistant and caregiver. In hindsight, it sounds like a second job, but as every son or daughter with an ailing parent knows, and though it is time-consuming, most days you don't even notice the time go by and even when you do there is nothing in the world you would rather be doing. So whether I was collecting his mail, chaperoning him to events or helping him get dressed, it was nothing more than he deserved.

As is typical of men and women of a certain age, Quentin talked a lot about his own death. When you are older and live alone, you have a lot of personal time and you drift in your thoughts. You start to think about how much time you have left. If you reach sixty, you realize death is probably twenty or so years away. When you're eighty, it is likely a lot closer. After Quentin turned eighty, he started talking more and more about death. His body was falling apart. His stage presence had always been full of energy, but the older he got, the more his exuberance declined. He frequently talked, on stage and off, about wanting to die because he could no longer live the way he wanted. When he turned ninety in December 1998, he openly wished that death would hurry up and arrive. By that time, he had cancer, a hernia, blood pressure problems, an enlarged heart, and debilitating eczema.

We had already begun to get his affairs in order. In other words, Quentin had started to physically prepare for his death. Sometime in 1997 he approached me with a request to help him write one final book. This was odd. Up until that point, Quentin had confessed to only ever writing books that were requested of him. This one would be different. This would be the first and only book he wanted to write. It would also be his last. In it, he wanted to voice all that he had left to say. His original idea was to call the book *The Dusty Answers*, a reference to the fact that we would record material for the proposed tome from the subject matters that arose from the Q&A portion of his one-man show. In the end though, since Quentin's purpose was to have the last word on his life, we went with a different, more appropriate title. For the next two years, Quentin and I would record our conversations, slowly creating the content that you have just read. We finished those sessions in July 1999, about four months before Quentin died.

Not long afterward, Quentin started to clear out the contents of his apartment, room five at 46 East 3rd Street. Now anyone that knew Quentin knows that this was extraordinary. Up until then, Quentin would not let anyone move anything in his room. His tiny residence was packed from wall to wall with bags of what to an outsider might look like junk or garbage. That was how Quentin lived. Despite the chaotic appearance however, Quentin knew where everything was, or would so as long as nothing was moved. From July, he started gathering things that we might consign to the trash. During that time I also helped him clear out the floor of his closet where he kept his paperwork. Eventually Quentin created a path from his front door into and around his room, a path that hitherto had never existed.

In his final months, Quentin also asked me to help him prepare a new will. Quentin had been perturbed by someone pressuring him to hand over his life's work and savings so they could "look after things for him." Quentin was having none of it. As part of our cleanup, we gathered together his old wills and found that a number of people named in the most recent version of his will were now dead. This prompted the creation of a new will that split his savings principally between his three nieces and left future revenue from his books to his collaborators and partners. He also left token sums of money to people he believed might think they deserved more substantial legacies, and whose potential pain he wanted to soothe. He signed the will one week to the day before his death.

When and how Quentin died is a matter of historical fact. Following the success of a revival of his one-man show, "An Evening with Quentin Crisp" at the Intar Theater, New York, beginning in 1998 to coincide with his ninetieth birthday, Quentin was offered the chance to take the show back to England. A number of people advised him against this, I being one of them. None of us were sure his body could survive the rigors such travel would place on it. Now, of course, we know that it couldn't. Nevertheless, Quentin was determined to go. It's worth asking why, since there are those who claim that Quentin effectively committed suicide by doing so.

Quentin was certainly aware of the possibility of his dying on the trip to England, but he didn't undertake the tour knowing with certainty that it would kill him. Yes, he is on record noting the merits of suicide for someone in his dilapidated condition. He also openly confessed to being physically incapable of taking his own life, not to mention mentally incapable of doing so – Quentin was a self-confessed "sissy" in that regard. So focusing on those two facts alone, one might conclude that a "suicide tour" was Quentin's best way out of this world. This was not the case. In truth, Quentin went to England for one reason and one reason only: he was a professional people person. He didn't want to let down the organizers of the tour, and he wouldn't have wanted to let down those who had bought tickets to see and hear him. Being on stage, having a voice, and being the center of attention was Quentin's lifeblood. It is what he lived for, and that's why he flew to England on November 20, 1999.

Partial proof of this can be seen in Quentin's reaction to the machinations of a so-called friend who had tried to cancel his upcoming tour of England "for Quentin's own good". I arrived at Quentin's apartment one evening having collected his mail. I had brought food for us both and assumed we would eat and go through his letters and fan mail together, as was our normal routine. I used my key to let myself into his apartment only to find Quentin uncharacteristically furious. He instantly accused me of being in league with this third person and of trying to ruin his livelihood. I assured him I had no part in it. He eventually calmed down, but behind his hostility was a determination that no person would conspire with his failing body to prevent him from doing exactly as he wished. I told Quentin that I only wanted what he wanted. He was ninety years old and had lived his entire life on his terms. Why should he stop now? I knew that Quentin might die on the trip to England, but in truth, he might have died at any moment of any number of things. He should just do what he wanted and what he wanted to do was go to England and be Quentin Crisp. That was what he lived for.

My partner and I dined with Quentin on the night before he left for England. I had already seen him twice that week, once to talk about work and on another occasion to give him his nitroglycerin pills (for his angina) which I had picked up from his local pharmacy. Quentin didn't want to take the pills in case they prolonged his life. I persuaded him that taking them would instead actually increase the quality of life he had left, and he seemed happy with that explanation and accepted them. I collected Quentin from his apartment on Thursday evening and we made our way to Haveli Banjara, a local Indian restaurant. While we waited for Charles to arrive, I helped Quentin study for the written test he planned to take as part of applying to become an American citizen. He got every answer right. Two of Quentin's remaining life ambitions were to become an American citizen and to meet Elizabeth Taylor.

Over dinner, Quentin talked about the passing of his life. I suspect he had received a phone call shortly before I arrived from someone making one last plea for him not to go to England. This had agitated him but as I have said before, death was also a topic that he had discussed both publicly and privately for many years at that point. One thing he did do at the end of the evening, which was out of character, was give me a publicity poster from his film *Orlando* that he had signed. It was not clear to me that was him saying goodbye, but we were both aware that dinner that night might be the last time we saw each other. After dinner, Charles and I walked Quentin back to his apartment building. As he pulled himself up the staircase with his right hand gripping the railing, I wished him the best for his tour and told Quentin I loved him, and as he slowly moved up the stairs he calmly and quietly told me he loved me. Then I waited in the lobby of his building and listened to him climb the stairs to his floor. Once I heard him arrive and shuffle toward his apartment door, we said goodnight.

The next morning I called him to wish him a safe flight. He was in good spirits. His journey to Manchester would take him first to London Heathrow and then immediately onwards on a second, shorter flight. That evening he stayed in the house of Emma Ferguson, a lady he had never met and a friend of a friend, a set-up arranged at Quentin's request by his tour's organizers, a situation that Quentin preferred to a hotel. The morning after his arrival in England on November 21, 1999, Chip Snell, Quentin's companion for the tour, found him dead in his room. Chip found him lying in his bed with the bottle of angina pills in his hand and several pills scattered over the bed. I found out that Quentin had died when someone called me from

England to ask if I had seen the news. I hadn't, but I quickly turned on CNN to confirm what had happened. Although news of Quentin's passing left me heartbroken, I can't say it surprised me because of all that I have said thus far. Quentin died of a heart attack.

As per his wishes, Quentin was cremated and his ashes delivered to me by Chip when he returned from England. Quentin had personally instructed me to throw them in the garbage can, but I confess that was one request of his that I could not carry out. The months and years that followed were hard for me not only because I had lost one of the people I loved most in the world, but because Quentin made me the executor of his estate. The man who professed no skills and claimed to be unemployable amassed a personal fortune well in excess of a million dollars during his lifetime. It just goes to show you how much you can save if you live as frugally as he did and never say no to an opportunity.

Charles and I spent the two months following Quentin's death emptying his apartment. In theory, we could have cleared it out in a day, given its small size, but that would have been careless not to mention practically impossible. For contrary to Quentin's assertion that, "After the first four years the dirt doesn't get any worse," eighteen years of dust and grime actually creates a considerable barrier and problem. Of course, Quentin was never troubled by it, but that's because he was wise enough never to move anything in his apartment. For us, it was a different story. The first day was the worst because we were not fully prepared. We lasted about two hours before retreating. Each of us had trouble breathing. When we came back thereafter, we brought protective masks and gloves. Oddly, while the dirt likely caused or aggravated Quentin's eczema, I'm convinced the conditions he lived in actually contributed to his longevity by boosting his immune system. By the time we were done with the room, the sink's color had changed from black back to white and the carpet, which was irreparable, had been removed.

Quentin wasn't a hoarder, despite the picture I've painted. You have to remember that his room was very small, so everything he owned was kept in that one room. What he did collect however were his manuscripts, books, photographs (principally of himself), magazines and newspaper articles as well as assorted items that had been gifted to him over the years. A beetle in a ring box. A piece of the Berlin Wall. Quentin had attempted to throw away a lot of his early photographs some months earlier, but I convinced him not to and offered to look after them instead. They seemed to make him feel bad because they showed him looking young and beautiful. Something that in his advanced age seemed alien to him.

As my co-editor mentioned in the foreword to this book, *The Last Word* is being published eighteen years to the day of Quentin's passing. Why has it taken so long to get it to you? Well, there are a number of reasons. In the years that followed Quentin's death, I busied myself with his estate as I have said. I am a meticulous person and wanted to make sure that Quentin's wishes were carried out to the letter and that his legacy was secured. Additionally, I helped arrange a memorial for Quentin, which was held at the Cooper Union on March 3, 2000. The principal reason for this book's delay however, is that *The Last Word* was created via a series of interviews that Quentin and I conducted and all of these had to be transcribed first before they could be edited. Initially, I couldn't even listen to Quentin's voice because of the heartache and tears that came with being transported back to each moment in time. We got there in the end, but I will admit it took a lot of time for me to heal.

What did Quentin mean to me? He was part of my life for thirteen years. In the end, I had a longer adult relationship with him than I did with my own mother and father, and for me, he fulfilled both of those roles. Had Quentin not been in my life it would have been quite different because my initial meeting with him on film gave me the affirmation I needed to be my true self. Without Quentin, I would not have set out on the journey of self-discovery that I did.

Being Quentin's friend provided me with many life experiences that I otherwise would not have had. Having him in my life, sharing his, and being worthy of his love made every day that I knew him like a fairy tale. It validated the influence the movie had on me as a young man. It reminded me and continues to remind me every day that it is okay to be me. If you take anything from Quentin's life and writing, it should be that the problem is never with you, it is with the outside world.

Taking on the responsibility for Quentin's estate after his death has been a mixed experience. On the positive side, I have learned a lot about the law and have been able to ensure that Quentin's final wishes were executed. I have also been able to preserve and prolong his influence. On the negative side, I have learned a lot about the users and hangers-on that were present in Quentin's life and who continued to make demands on him long after his death.

Quentin became part of my family. One of the truly beautiful aspects of the gay community is our notion of the family you choose versus the family you are born with. For many of us who have struggled with families that are unaccepting of our sexuality, this is the lemonade we make from the lemons life gives us. Quentin was someone whom I loved unconditionally, and I grieved for him like a lost parent when he died. Quentin *was* family.

I am thrilled that *The Last Word* is finally published. I'm also relieved to finally let go of the guilt that I have felt all the time it remained unpublished. *The Last Word* compliments *The Naked Civil Servant* because, like the former, it too has a certain sadness, though a sadness absent of self-pity. The thing I am delighted about most however, is knowing that there are people out there who will now fall in love with Quentin all over again.

Phillip Ward
October 2017

59879354R00128